Rain On a Beautiful Day

By

Kovan L. White

Acknowledgments

Michael Owen – Project Manager

Jannet Rogers – Project Manager

Ana Abby – Editor and Formatter

Irene Park – HOD

Adam – Designer

Table of Contents

INTRODUCTION:

THE SPARK THAT FUELED THE

FLAMES

In this book, you will find not only the poem that ignited my passion for writing but also a collection of others that have shaped my journey. They are surrounded by the details of the events that inspired them, the moments of joy and heartbreak, triumph, and defeat that have marked my life.

At the end of the main story, you will discover additional poems that explain the backstory of my life in the Prequel. They are memories, events, moments turned into short stories.

I hope that as you read the pages of this book, you will find comfort, inspiration, and perhaps a reflection of your own experiences within these words. May these words resonate with your heart, for it is in sharing our stories that we truly come alive.

The journey began in Middle School; the eighth-grade English teacher had given the class a simple task to write a poem. It seemed like such a straightforward assignment, but for Kovan, it was a daunting challenge. Words didn't come easily to him, and the idea of expressing his thoughts and emotions felt like an insurmountable task. Yet, there he was, clutching my paper, ready to share his creation with the class.

As the teacher announced she was about to read his poem he could feel the eyes of his classmates on him, their gazes filled with curiosity. His heart pounded in his chest, and a sheen of sweat formed on his forehead. The poem went as follows.

Introduction

POEM

The Sun Will Soon Rise Again
The sun rises and falls
The beauty takes us all
The birds and bees all fling about
But the night is soon to come
The mountains and trees all covered in black
As the moon tries to take it back
But the sun will soon rise again
And shine the day
As the moon fades away

As she finished reading the last line, the classroom fell silent. Kovan looked around, searching for a reaction. The teacher's eyes sparkled with delight, and a smile graced her lips. She applauded, breaking the stillness. The sound of clapping hands filled the room.

The teacher's voice cut through the applause, "Well done Kovan! Let's give a round of applause to our talented poet!" Her words were met with cheers and applause, but a hint of disbelief hung in the air. It seemed that my classmates couldn't fathom that such words could have originated from him.

The feeling of embarrassment washed over him. He had poured everything into those verses, and yet it seemed inconceivable to some of his peers that he could have created something so profound. In their eyes, Kovan was guilty of plagiarizing the work of a more skilled poet.

But looking back now, he realized that their disbelief was a compliment in disguise. It meant that his words had transcended their expectations. The power of poetry has allowed him to connect with others in ways he had never imagined possible.

CHAPTER 1:

CHANGING WINDS

It all began one summer afternoon, as the bus rumbled along, carrying Kovan and my cousin Kevin to football practice. We were sitting at the back of the bus, as it was the prime spot to claim in our day and age. Little did he know that this seemingly ordinary bus ride would mark the beginning of a series of unexpected encounters and experiences.

Kovan gazed out the window, oblivious to the world around him. Meanwhile, his cousin noticed two familiar faces from his high school—two girls who were on their way to track practice. They happened to be a grade ahead of Kovan, heading into the tenth grade. Engrossed in their conversation, Kovan barely acknowledged their presence.

However, one of the girls seemed determined to break through his aloofness. She made an effort to strike up a conversation with him, undeterred by his lack of interest.

Despite his short and somewhat standoffish responses, she persisted, asking for his name. He curtly replied, "Kovan," confirming that he was indeed Kevin's cousin. She continued with her inquiries, asking where they were headed, to which he simply answered, "Practice." Though his demeanor may have seemed rude, he wasn't intentionally trying to be. He was just in his own world.

Finally, the bus arrived at our stop, and Kovan breathed a sigh of relief. He was free from Miss "I-don't-even-remember-her-name." Little did he know that this encounter was merely a prelude to the transformative experiences that awaited him.

The first day of football practice arrived, and Kovan found myself donning football pads for the very first time. Fear gripped him, as he stepped onto the field with trepidation. In his neighborhood, he was a backyard legend, emulating the skills of football greats like Jerry Rice, Deion Sanders, and Steve Young. He boasted about having the best hands in all of southern California. But now, surrounded by my peers in full gear, doubts crept in, and he questioned his own abilities.

Kovan harbored a deep-seated fear. It gripped him tightly, making his heart race and his palms sweat. Every time he stepped onto the practice field, the fear of getting hit paralyzed him. Despite his dedication and passion for the game, Kovan couldn't shake off this nagging apprehension.

However, it wasn't just the fear of physical impact that troubled him. Kovan couldn't fathom why, despite his love for the game and his unwavering commitment, he seemed to be consistently overlooked by the coaches. He watched as less talented players secured positions ahead of him, wondering why his abilities went unnoticed. It was a question that gnawed at his mind, leaving him with a mix of frustration and self-doubt.

But Kovan was determined. The love he held for the game burned brighter than ever, fueling his unwavering dedication. He couldn't simply give up on his dreams because of the obstacles in his path. With resilience and a determination to prove himself, he made up his mind to stick with it, to persevere despite the setbacks. Yet, despite his best efforts, his moment of recognition eluded him.

However, Kovan refused to let bitterness consume him. Instead, he chose to focus on the sheer joy that the game brought him. Every time he stepped onto the field, he embraced the rush of adrenaline that surged through his veins. The sound of cleats on grass, the feel of the ball in his hands.

Through it all, Kovan remained committed to his team's success, regardless of his own position within it. He cheered his teammates on, offering words of encouragement and support. Despite his own frustrations, he understood that the game was bigger than any individual player. His love for the sport transcended personal glory, driving him to contribute to the team's triumph in any way he could.

As the summer drew to a close, the beginning of high school loomed ahead. Kovan was entering a new chapter with a mixture of nervous excitement and curiosity. While education was certainly a part of it, he couldn't help but anticipate the choices and opportunities that awaited him in the realm of romance. He wasn't the player type, he longed for companionship, seeking that feeling of connection and love.

Little did he know that the journey through high school would offer far more than just academic growth. It would become a time of self-discovery, of forging friendships and relationships, and of embracing unexpected experiences that would shape the person he was to become.

Just as the summer was coming to a close, an unexpected phone call added to the confusion of those final days. It was a prank call orchestrated by an old girlfriend, who enlisted the help of her friend to test my reaction. Little did he know this phone call would introduce him to someone who would become an integral part of his life—Patrice.

After the conversation with his ex-girlfriend's friend ended, the phone rang again, but this time it was Patrice on the line, without his ex-girlfriend present. Patrice, who was in the same grade as him but had attended a different middle school, entered his life as a friend, and that friendship would continue to grow.

Although Patrice saw our connection in a romantic light, Kovan saw her more as a sister. Nevertheless, she remained a loyal and steadfast friend throughout their years together. Their bond was strong, yet both of them possessed stubborn streaks that often led to prolonged periods of silence when they were upset with each other. It seemed that one of those silent periods was about to begin.

As the summer came to an end and school started, the tension between Patrice and Kovan lingered. Their disagreement had driven a wedge between them, and they embarked on one of their infamous months-long bouts of not speaking. It was a pattern they would fall into time and time again—closing themselves off, nursing their wounded pride, and allowing time to heal the wounds.

However, even during these periods of silence, their connection remained palpable. They were both aware of the absence of their friendship, and it weighed on them. Despite the temporary rift, Kovan knew deep down that Patrice was a great friend, fiercely loyal and always there when he needed her. Their disagreements may have caused temporary rifts, but they were mere bumps on the road that ultimately strengthened our bond.

As the weeks turned into months, the silence between them stretched on. They started to miss each other's presence, the camaraderie, and the support that came with their friendship. And slowly, almost imperceptibly, they began to bridge the gap that had formed between them.

Looking back on those moments, Kovan realized that their friendship was built on a foundation of resilience. They had weathered previous storms, and this time would be no different. The stubbornness that once kept them apart would eventually bring them back together.

Little did he know that this period of silence would mark a turning point in their friendship. It would serve as a reminder of the value we placed on each other's presence in their lives. And when the time came for them to reconcile, their friendship would emerge stronger than ever, ready to face the challenges that lay ahead.

POEM

It seemed like yesterday when you first called me on the phone
After that moment, I thought about it all night long
You could tell by my response when I came back with the baby
bottle
Huffing and puffing as if I'd just won the lotto
After all our arguments, I felt that I'd won
For months we wouldn't speak, you never know what you have until
it's done
Remember all our late-night games
Nothing else compares, I felt I had fame
Sometimes I ponder what might have been
But the only thing in my mind involved sin

Rain On A Beautiful Day

I know there's a lot of substance our relationship lacked
But through it all, you always had my back
There's a few times I told you what you've meant to me
You still and always will be the most important person to me
Having special friends like you is very much underrated
What a beautiful friend you are, I just feel so elated
Patrice, you sure are one of a kind
In my heart, you'll always be mine.

CHAPTER 2:

HOLE IN MY POCKET

Amidst the tangled web of friendships and shifting dynamics, another figure emerged in the story—Taneesha, the girl whose constant presence had become an incessant reminder of Miss "I don't even remember your name." Taneesha's greetings filled every corner of Kovan's school day, echoing relentlessly in his ears.

For three months straight, Taneesha's voice permeated every moment of Kovan's school life. Whether it was in the morning, during nutrition breaks, or at lunch, her enthusiastic "Hi Kovan'' seemed to follow him everywhere. The repetition became maddening, testing Kovan's patience. He longed for a respite from the relentless salutations.

Yet, as fate would have it, one day the familiar greeting ceased. Taneesha was no longer there to greet him at school, nor did she appear during lunchtime. It was as if she had vanished from his every waking moment. And that's when Kovan realized something unexpected—he started to miss her.

Thoughts of Taneesha occupied his mind more and more, as he pondered the significance of her absence. But he soon discovered that Taneesha had already moved on, not necessarily with another guy, but from him specifically. She had drawn her own conclusions and decided to distance herself. Perhaps she had finally understood Kovan's lack of interest.

In the midst of reflecting on Taneesha's departure, Kovan came to a profound realization. Unbeknownst to him, he had an empty frame within his life, waiting to be filled. Taneesha's presence had occupied that frame, leaving a void when she departed. It became clear to Kovan that she held a special place in his heart, even though he had failed to recognize it earlier.

As time went on, Kovan understood the depth of his feelings for Taneesha. He yearned for the return of her cheerful greetings and the connection they had shared. But sometimes, it takes the absence of someone to truly appreciate their presence. The empty frame that once went unnoticed now served as a reminder of the impact Taneesha had on Kovan's life.

Though their paths had diverged, hoped that one day, their paths would intersect once more, allowing him to fill the empty frame with the warmth and joy only Taneesha could bring.

The tables had turned, and it was now Kovan who approached Taneesha with greetings and anticipation for their encounters. Initially, she played hard to get, but eventually, they became boyfriend and girlfriend.

POEM

The first day we meet will be forever frozen in time
Who knew, a few months later you'll soon be mine
I tried to blow you off but man you sure were fine
I may have been young, a little stupid but I wasn't blind
I was entering high school ready for anything it would bring
But for the first three months you were the only person I seen
Hi Kovan-hi Kovan, man this girl won't let me breathe
Who knew that Taneesha, Taneesha
Would be the only word my heart sings
Hold on I'm getting ahead of myself
I started to see the beauty that was within
With you by my side, this game of love I'll surely win
A girl with intelligence and class, is what I hoped would come true
Once I found it, I couldn't handle it because I was intimidated by
you

One vivid memory stood out in Kovan's mind, a moment when he visited Taneesha at her home. Naively, he had chosen to wear red sweats in a neighborhood where the local gang held a strong aversion to the color red. As fate would have it, an older gangster confronted him, demanding to know where he was from. Kovan, in his innocence and fear, responded with the full name of his hometown, Pasadena, California, and its zip code, 91103.

Meanwhile, Kovan's best friend, Patrice, returned to the picture, filled with frustration and disappointment over his newfound relationship with Taneesha. Despite her feelings, Patrice chose to remain a friend, perhaps hoping that one day Kovan would see her in a different light. Their friendship endured, but the dynamics had shifted, complicated by unspoken desires and unrequited feelings.

Kovan struggled with a peculiar affliction that held him back from truly expressing his emotions. Being in groups paralyzed him, preventing his true personality from shining through. The one person whom Kovan desperately wanted to break free from his shell was Taneesha, the girl he loved more than anything in the world.

Kovan yearned for love and affection, but his fear crippled him. Whenever he was with Taneesha, they appeared more like friends than a couple. Countless times, Kovan would gaze into Taneesha's eyes, overcome by the desire to lean in and kiss her. However, his fear was an invisible barrier that held his body back, rendering him incapable of taking that leap.

Taneesha was patient and understanding but could she sense Kovan's struggle? She saw the depth of his feelings through his eyes, but she yearned for the affection that remained just out of reach. As days turned into weeks, and weeks turned into months, she couldn't help but question how long she could hold on to a relationship devoid of physical and emotional intimacy. The absence of passion left a void that neither of them could ignore.

Kovan pondered these thoughts every single day, tormented by his own limitations. He yearned to break free from his self-imposed prison and show Taneesha the depth of his love. The weight of his own insecurities began to take a toll on him, gnawing at his spirit. Each day, he beat himself up, frustrated by his inability to be the partner Taneesha deserved.

Taneesha had reached a breaking point. She had held on to the relationship for as long as she could, hoping that Kovan would break free from his fear and show her the love and affection she craved.

Her heart heavy with sadness and longing, Taneesha knew she had to make a difficult decision. She deserved to be with someone who could reciprocate her love and affection. She couldn't continue depriving herself of the intimacy and passion that she desired in a relationship. With a heavy heart, she mustered the courage to end things with Kovan.

Taneesha spent countless hours contemplating her decision. She paced back and forth, her mind flooded with memories of their time together. It was not an easy choice, but she had to prioritize her own happiness and well-being. She knew that staying in a relationship devoid of affection would only lead to more pain and dissatisfaction in the long run.

Summoning her strength, Taneesha sat down with Kovan one day, their favorite spot in the park now heavy with the weight of the impending conversation. With tears welling up in her eyes, she expressed her feelings honestly and openly. She explained how she yearned for a deeper connection, for a love that would encompass both emotional and physical intimacy.

Kovan, taken aback by Taneesha's words, realized the depth of the pain he had caused her. He understood that his fear had kept him from being the partner she needed and deserved. His heart sank as he realized the consequences of his actions, or rather, his lack of action.

Although devastated, Kovan respected Taneesha's decision. He acknowledged that he had failed to give her the love and affection she craved, and he couldn't blame her for walking away. Deep down, he knew that she deserved happiness and fulfillment.

And so, with a heavy heart and a bittersweet farewell, Taneesha and Kovan parted ways. Each of them carried the memories of their time together, the lessons learned, and the pain of what could have been.

And so, their paths diverged, leading them on separate journeys of growth and self-realization. The story of Kovan and Taneesha, only lasting the entirety of his freshman year, serves as a reminder that sometimes, love alone is not enough to sustain a relationship. It requires mutual effort, vulnerability, and the willingness to confront one's fears. Their story, although short-lived, left an indelible mark on their hearts, guiding them toward a future where they would both find the love and passion they truly deserved.

The traumas of his past, the screams from his mother during his father's abusive episodes, had left deep scars on his psyche, altering his once outgoing and carefree personality. Kovan firmly believed that these traumatic experiences had shaped his identity, turning him into a closed-off and reserved individual with frayed nerves.

Even minor conflicts or confrontations at school would trigger intense fear and anxiety within him. His heart would race, his body would sweat, and a sense of overwhelming dread would consume him. This internal struggle often led to a short temper and an increased susceptibility to frustration and annoyance.

Reading in front of others became a tremendous challenge for Kovan. The simple act of speaking simple words like "it," "the," and "was" seemed to escape his comprehension. The memories of struggling in grade school resurfaced, prompting him to avoid reading aloud whenever possible. At times, he would become so zoned out and disconnected from his surroundings that he remained entirely unaware of his own detachment.

While Kovan could vividly recall the struggles he faced, he found it difficult to recall many other events he had experienced. The scars of his past had etched themselves deeply into his memory, leaving him with a fragmented recollection of his life.

With each passing day, Kovan grappled with the lasting impact of his childhood traumas, as they continued to shape his present reality. He yearned for a sense of peace and a release from the anxieties that plagued him, hoping that one day he could rediscover the outgoing, fun-loving personality he was meant to have.

POEM

Seems like I was born to lose from the beginning
Since I was a seed my pop's he wasn't winning
Against the drug game, soon after all the problems began
We felt the effects wondering how long it would remain
Can you delete my memories...running to grandma's house?
Can still see her expression inquiring what is this all about
Can still see the tears; till this day makes me want to shout
Can still feel the fears; like being thrown in a heavyweight bout
Kids at a young age they soak in everything they see
Abusing your spouse is that the way it's supposed to be
A house with no love is that the future set for me
It's breaking me down I see nowhere for me to flee
My nerves are shot; would shake every time I see pops
Would call the cops just wishing that the drama would stop
I'm not joking, any commotion rather big or small
My heart jumps out of my chest like seeing Biggy fall
I can't say he didn't show me anything he showed me the nots'
Not a lot, listen again, I said he showed me the nots'
How not to be a husband also how not to be a pops
How not to love your kids and how not to be on top
Let me stop now that I think about it. He showed me a lot...Dang
Pop!

CHAPTER 3:

SUNSHINE GRAY SKIES

Years later, after much introspection and self-reflection, and with this newfound understanding, Kovan acknowledged the impact all this had on his past relationship with Taneesha. As their connection deteriorated, feelings of guilt consumed him. He couldn't blame her for wanting to end their relationship, as he himself recognized the friend in boyfriend's clothing he had become. It was clear that Taneesha had grown tired of the superficiality and lack of emotional depth that characterized their romance.

Kovan's life took an unexpected turn when he met Taneesha. Her brightness and kind-heartedness helped him relax more. Her presence was an escape from the pains of his home life. Now that she's gone, he has no safe place to run.

Seeing Taneesha around school became an agonizing experience for Kovan. The sight of her joyful smile, which he once cherished, made him start avoiding her, choosing to take different routes whenever he caught a glimpse of her approaching. The mornings that used to bring excitement for school turned into moments of dread, and Kovan found it increasingly difficult to focus on his studies.

Even during football practice, his performance began to suffer. The passion and drive that once fueled him now wavered as his mind became consumed by remorse. His teammates noticed his distracted state, but Kovan couldn't bring himself to explain the cause of his turmoil. The worst part for Kovan was that he knew he was solely responsible for the pain he felt and the distance between himself and Taneesha. He longed for a chance to make amends, to rectify his mistake.

While Kovan held no resentment towards Taneesha for moving on, he couldn't help but feel a surge of anger when he discovered that she had started dating Donald, a fellow teammate from their football team. The sight of them together at school and during practices felt like a painful stab to his heart. In the realm of their shared football brotherhood, where camaraderie and loyalty were supposed to prevail, the intrusion of a romantic relationship shattered the illusion of solidarity.

Donald had betrayed him by pursuing Taneesha, the very person Kovan held dear. The news struck Kovan like a lightning bolt, shaking the foundation of his trust and igniting a fire of anger within him. The tension at football practice became visible, casting a dark cloud over the once joyful bond between the teammates. Laughter turned into clenched jaws and terse conversations. The unity they had once shared on the field began to crumble under the weight of betrayal.

Kovan couldn't fathom why Donald would break the unwritten rule that existed among teammates—a rule that demanded loyalty and respect, not only for the game but for each other's personal boundaries. The betrayal cut deep, raising questions about the authenticity of their loyalty and leaving Kovan wrestling with conflicting emotions.

His mind wandered during drills continuously, his once-sharp instincts dulled by the turmoil within. Yes, the game that used to bring him solace now became a battlefield of conflicting emotions.

But amid the chaos, Kovan's resolve remained unwavering. He refused to let anger consume him entirely. Deep down, he knew that the situation demanded more than vengeance or a further spiral into bitterness. He needed to find a way to navigate through the storm and rise above the turmoil.

In that moment, Kovan's anger began to ebb away, replaced by a mixture of compassion and understanding. He recognized that Taneesha was not his enemy. They both had made mistakes, navigating the intricate web of emotions in the aftermath of their shattered relationship.

POEM

A man's pain
She was my love; I needed nothing and no more to gain
But when respect is lost you surely see a man's pain
Sometimes I wonder what love is really about
I'm not going to give up
Because one day I'm going to certainly find out
Poem
I can't explain why I'm trying to be different not trying to be hard
I've done spent my whole life trying to cover my scars
I've been held so high now I'm afraid to expose my flaws
If life was the game of golf I'm just struggling to save par
I'm not your average Joe so people call me weird
They can say whatever they want I'll never shed a tear
You see this is Satan's earth so I don't belong here
I know the true of Jah so I have no fears
Since I'm not a part of this world I tend to feel so lonely
So I need someone not to physical but mentally hold me
When it's time to give in, it seems they try to control me
So just leave me alone because I'm good on my own
They say that I'm quiet, but I don't pay them no mind
I observe my surroundings as I stay on the grind
For the fools on this earth, I just don't have any time
Call me stuck up all you want, but just don't cross the line

As time went on, their ill-fated relationship began to crumble, and Taneesha's connection with Donald proved short-lived. Meanwhile, Kovan remained single throughout his sophomore year, unwilling to settle for just anybody. He desired a sense of freedom and a genuine connection, but his heart still yearned for the familiarity and depth he had experienced with Taneesha. No one could measure up, and no one seemed to pan out as a suitable replacement. In his eyes, no one could compare to Taneesha, and his longing for her persisted.

Now a junior in high school, Kovan carried the weight of his past experiences with him. The memories of his failed relationship and the sense of inadequacy lingered, leaving him feeling lost and devoid of purpose. Despite his desire for companionship, he hesitated to pursue new romantic interests, fearing that they would fall short of the connection he had once shared with Taneesha. The absence of love and the ongoing search for someone who could measure up left him feeling miserable and yearning for the depth and authenticity that had eluded him thus far.

As Patrice observed Kovan's lingering heartache and vulnerability, she saw an opportunity for them to finally be together. In her mind, this was the perfect moment for their friendship to transition into something more. Patrice possessed beauty, sweetness, and genuine affection for Kovan. However, despite her admirable qualities, there was an intangible force that kept Kovan from reciprocating her feelings. That force was none other than his unwavering love for Taneesha. Kovan was determined to win her back and reignite their connection.

His quest to rekindle their romance began by reestablishing their friendship. They spent time together, exploring different places and creating new memories. It felt like they were the only two people in the world, encapsulated within a one hundred-mile radius of adventure.

Determined to make amends for the love and affection he had denied her in their past, Kovan set out to show Taneesha the depths of his love. One particular memory loomed large in Kovan's mind—their very first kiss. It had remained a liberating moment frozen in time, forever etched in his heart. Now, with a newfound clarity and determination, he saw this moment as a chance for redemption, a chance to right the wrongs that had haunted him.

It was a cloudy day when they found themselves waiting for the bus after spending time at the mall. As light rain began to fall, a gentle mist filled the air, casting a sense of enchantment over the surroundings. Kovan's heart raced as he looked into Taneesha's eyes, just as he had done during their first go-around.

This time, he knew it would be different. With every ounce of courage within him, Kovan leaned in, closing the distance between their lips and kissed her. The world seemed to stand still as their breaths intertwined, creating a moment that was electric. It was a kiss that spoke volumes, carrying with it the weight of redemption, forgiveness of oneself.

In that moment, Kovan felt an overwhelming sense of relief. It washed over him like a warm wave, soothing the doubts and insecurities that had plagued him for so long. The weight he had carried on his shoulders was lifted, replaced by a profound sense of accomplishment. He had mustered the strength to seize the moment, to embrace the vulnerability that comes with expressing true affection.

As they pulled away, their lips parting, a newfound serenity settled upon them. The light rain continued to fall, its delicate droplets serving as a symbol of renewal and cleansing. Kovan's heart swelled with relief, a relief that surpassed mere joy. It was a relief born from the knowledge that he had finally acted on his true feelings, that he had taken a step towards rectifying the mistakes of the past.

For months, he had carried a void in his heart, longing for the one girl who had once completed his life—Taneesha. She was back in Kovan's life. Realizing the moment set off fireworks erupted within his heart. The empty spaces that had long plagued him suddenly overflowed with warmth and joy. It was as if the universe had conspired to grant him a second chance at happiness.

As Kovan embraced Taneesha, the world around them seemed to transform. The scent of blooming flowers carried a sweeter fragrance, and the flavors of food danced on his tongue with newfound intensity. The rain that gently fell from the sky turned into a shower of lemon drops and gumdrops, immersing them in a whimsical enchantment.

Their reunion was a blend of laughter and tears, as they relived cherished memories and exchanged stories of the time they had spent apart. The scars of their past began to heal, and hope blossomed within their souls. Kovan knew that he had finally gotten his baby back—the missing piece of his heart.

With their love reignited, Kovan and Taneesha embarked on a journey of rediscovery. They rekindled the flame that had once burned brightly, nurturing it with patience, understanding, and unwavering devotion.

Every passing day brought them closer, and Kovan marveled at the transformation that had occurred within his heart. With Taneesha by his side, the world felt vibrant and alive. The simplest moments became infused with magic and wonder. They explored new horizons, created memories that would last a lifetime, and cherished every breath they took together.

Their love not only completed Kovan's life but also propelled them to become the best versions of themselves. Taneesha's unwavering support and understanding helped Kovan realize his true potential. Their bond grew stronger with time, and the flames of puppy love were rekindled. But not everyone celebrated their newfound happiness.

Enter Patrice, who found herself trapped in a whirlwind of conflicting emotions. She couldn't bear to witness Kovan and Taneesha's joy, as it shattered her own desires for a romantic connection with him. Unwilling to endure the pain of unrequited love, she initiated yet another breakup with Kovan, stepping back from their friendship in an effort to protect her own heart.

The complexities of love and friendship intertwined, creating a delicate dance of emotions and desires. Kovan's heart remained steadfast in its pursuit of Taneesha, while Patrice found herself grappling with her unfulfilled longing. The journey of self-discovery, romantic entanglements, and personal growth continued, with each character navigating their own path through the intricate web of teenage relationships.

CHAPTER 4:

TOP TO BOTTOM

Kovan vividly recalled the cherished moment when Taneesha first confessed her love for him. It was an evening filled with thoughts consumed by her presence. With a nostalgic smile, he remembered the ingenious way he decided to communicate his affection to her—through a voice message on the pager. In those days, pagers were the epitome of modern communication.

Preparing himself for this pivotal moment, Kovan carefully lined up his Blackstreet cassette, ensuring that everything was just right. He played the intro, savoring the soulful melody, and then paused the tape. In that brief pause, he expressed his feelings. With a touch of nervous excitement, he simply said, "Hey Taneesha, just thinking about you. Have a good night and see you tomorrow."

Little did he know that his simple message would elicit such a profound response. Taneesha, moved by his words and the depth of their connection, promptly returned his call. The words she spoke next filled his heart with overwhelming joy and reassurance: "I think I love you." Overwhelmed with emotion, Kovan didn't hesitate for a second. "I love you too," he responded, sealing their bond in that heartfelt exchange.

In that blissful moment, everything felt right. Their love radiated, casting a warm glow over their world. It was as if nothing could go wrong, and a sense of contentment enveloped them. The echoes of their "I love yous" reverberated, encapsulating a chapter in their journey filled with hope, affection, and the promise of a future together.

POEM

What do you know, lightning does strike twice
It seems I won it all with one roll of the dice
Because the best thing that ever happened to me is back in my life
Remember the first time you said I love you
It was after I left that message with Blackstreet playing in the
background
It filled my heart with so much joy I'll never get used to hearing that
sound
By us falling in love, it officially made us high school sweethearts
I'm sorry for pressuring you to do the things that are usually done in
the dark
I'm now in the 11th grade, you've entered your senior year
What was to become of us after high school? That was my biggest
fear

During a challenging time in their relationship, a minor obstacle threatened to disrupt Kovan's communication with Taneesha. The unexpected turn of events occurred when his house phone was unexpectedly turned off. To Kovan, it felt as if his world was about to crumble. How could he possibly communicate with his beloved? Panic set in as he searched for alternative ways to reach her.

In his desperate pursuit to find a solution, Kovan ran a guilt trip on his mother. He hoped to make her understand the gravity of the situation and feel remorse for the inconvenience caused. Didn't she realize that her son was deeply in love? Doubts began to creep into his mind—was this a deliberate plot orchestrated by his own mother to break them apart? The thought lingered, and he contemplated the dynamics of keeping friends close and family even closer.

Regardless of the truth behind the phone disconnection, Kovan refused to let anything stand in the way of his connection with Taneesha. Determination fueled his actions as he discovered an alternative means of communication. Living near a park that had a payphone, he harnessed every opportunity to make a connection. Night after night, he would eagerly run to the park, coins in hand, ready to exchange them for precious minutes to speak with his high school sweetheart.

Amidst it all, Kovan found himself perplexed by his mother's choice of words. She referred to Taneesha as his "ball and chain." The reason behind this nickname remained a mystery to him, a puzzle he couldn't solve. Yet, it didn't deter him from pursuing his love and maintaining a steadfast bond with Taneesha. He remained resolute in his efforts, undeterred by external opinions or obstacles, with the sole focus of keeping their connection alive and flourishing.

As the end of the school year approached, uncertainty loomed over Kovan and Taneesha's future. The excitement of prom had faded, and the reality of their different paths became evident. Taneesha, having graduated, was ready to embark on her college journey, while Kovan had one more year remaining in high school. Deep down, they both knew that their lives were taking separate directions, and Taneesha didn't want to hold him back from his own opportunities.

Although Kovan agreed with her reasoning, a profound sadness overwhelmed his heart. The thought of being without her was painful, and he couldn't help but feel a sense of longing for the future they had envisioned together. Taneesha proposed a plan—reuniting in ten years. To Kovan, it seemed like an eternity. The emotional toll of waiting for a decade seemed unbearable, and he couldn't help but yearn for a shorter timeframe, perhaps just ten days, to ease his heartache.

With Taneesha off to college, Kovan found himself navigating his senior year without her by his side. He held onto a glimmer of hope that she would return to him someday, refusing to let go completely. Their attempts to remain friends proved challenging. Kovan would call her dorm

room, hoping to hear her voice on the other end, but more often than not, she wasn't available. The distance and the demands of their respective lives took a toll on their connection.

In the aftermath of their attempt to be friends, Kovan's mind became a battlefield of insecurities and doubts. Dark thoughts crept in, whispering unsettling questions about Taneesha's whereabouts and the people she associated with. His love, once a beacon of warmth, began to morph into an ugly shade of hate.

With each passing day, Kovan's mistrust grew, fueled by his overactive imagination. Whenever Taneesha was unavailable or failed to answer his calls, his mind conjured up scenarios of betrayal and deceit. The pain within him festered, turning their friendship into a toxic cycle of bitterness and resentment.

Whenever Taneesha reached out to him, hoping to share a laugh or find support from their connection, Kovan couldn't help but lash out. He responded with harshness, his words dripping with venom, as if hoping to push her away. The pain within him had clouded his judgment, convincing him that severing ties with Taneesha would somehow alleviate his anguish.

As days turned into weeks, their friendship eroded further, leaving behind a trail of hurt and confusion. The pain that Kovan had hoped to escape only intensified, leaving him feeling lonelier than ever. He had unknowingly become a victim of his own bitterness, closing himself off from the one person who had once been a source of comfort.

Deep down, Kovan knew that his actions were unfair and unjust. He recognized that the hatred he felt was merely a manifestation of his own unresolved pain and insecurities. It was not Taneesha's actions that had caused this anguish but his own distorted perception. But the damage was done, Kovan accomplished his goal of pushing Taneesha away.

POEM

Why must all good things come to an end?
But I thought with you, this game of love I was supposed to win
With you out of my life, the 12th grade was like a dream
No not one of those happy ones either, a nightmare is what it seemed
With my heart broken hopelessness is creeping near and nearer
I never thought I'd find myself crying in this mirror
It's been over a year and I'm still not over you
My skies are so gray, has the sun betrayed me too?
Please shine on me send me someone new
I was a finely crafted chair missing one little screw
I tried to hide it, but deep down inside that screw was you

POEM

I don't know where to go, so I'm gonna stop right here
I don't know what to say, so I'm gonna start right here
I don't know where to go, so I'm gonna park right here
I don't know what to do, only you can stop these tears
I don't know where to go
I don't know how to be
I don't know how to eat if you're not here with me
Feels like I lost my mind
When you walked out of my life
Was I standing in your way?
College girl was ready to play
Left me alone so cold
Felt like I was going insane
I was losing my brain
Don't want to hear your name
Don't want to see your face
Or drive by your place
Tell me why I can't move on
When it's you that did me wrong
Was my love for you too strong
A part of me just won't come home
The best part of me ain't coming home
Baby, won't you come back home
I don't know where to go, so I'm gonna stop right here
I don't know what to say, so I'm gonna start right here
I don't know where to go, so I'm gonna park right here
I don't know what to do, only you can stop these tears
I don't know where to go
I don't know how to be
I don't know how to eat when you're not here with me
Where did we go wrong?
Bring my baby home
Why did you run from me?
Trapped in these four walls like it's meant to be
Went from my former love to an enemy
Stuck between these lines like a harmony
Need a pharmacy

Rain On A Beautiful Day

For this pain you see
Crying out real loud
But you can't hear
Or you won't hear me
Did you move on from me?

Kovan realized that waiting around for someone who may or may not return wasn't the best course of action. He made a decision to move forward with his own life, refusing to let his world revolve solely around the hope of Taneesha's eventual return. It was a difficult choice, but a necessary one for his own well-being.

As prom approached, Kovan found himself not attending the grand event. In his heart, he held onto the belief that it was Taneesha's absence that prevented him from partaking in the festivities. Though the truth was more complex—financial constraints played a role as well—Kovan clung to the narrative that she was the reason he didn't go, allowing himself a sense of closure, a scapegoat for his disappointment.

The pain of feeling abandoned and left to fend for himself consumed Kovan's young heart. It was a profound low point in his life, as if he had been cast out into the wilderness without any guidance or support. The sense of being lost and alone was overwhelming, and he couldn't help but harbor resentment towards Taneesha for the pain she had caused him.

Once again, school no longer held the same significance, and even football couldn't fill the void left by Taneesha's absence. The pain and resentment had hardened his heart, and he wanted nothing more than to move on from Taneesha and erase her from his life.

CHAPTER 5:

CLOSE ENCOUNTER

As his senior year drew to a close, Kovan allowed himself to entertain the idea of exploring a connection with someone new. In one of his classes, he met Erin, a Hispanic girl who intrigued him with her air of mystery. She seemed to appear out of nowhere, despite attending the same class all along.

Erin seemed to radiate a vibrant energy. Though their interactions were limited to small talk, Kovan felt an undeniable spark, something new and different that breathed life into his weary soul. With each passing conversation, Kovan's spirit reenergized. Erin's presence ignited a fire within him, and he found himself looking forward to each day, eager for the opportunity to engage in more meaningful exchanges. The attention she bestowed upon him acted as a battery, fueling his enthusiasm and infusing his days with a newfound sense of purpose.

The school days that had once been mundane and monotonous now held the promise of excitement and anticipation fueled by the prospect of engaging with Erin.

Erin's zest for life was infectious, and Kovan found himself feeling alive in her presence. The walls that had confined him began to crumble.

Their friendship became a safe haven, a place where they could be vulnerable and genuine, supporting each other through the highs and lows of life.

In the hallways, Kovan no longer felt invisible. He walked with a renewed sense of confidence, a smile on his face, and a skip in his step. The vibrant energy between him and Erin was palpable, and their friendship blossomed, intertwining their lives in ways neither could have anticipated.

In the midst of their growing connection, Kovan never forgot the lessons he had learned from his past experiences. To show love and affection, to cherish the value of open communication, trust. The pain he had once felt had taught him to tread carefully, ensuring that his newfound friendship with Erin flourished in a healthy and balanced manner.

All good things must come to an end as Erin soon relocated to North Carolina. With Erin's departure, their contact dwindled, reduced to sporadic letters exchanged over time. The connection they had started to form was left hanging, the distance between them making it difficult to maintain regular communication. Despite the brief encounter, Erin left a lasting impression on Kovan, further reinforcing the notion that there might be possibilities beyond Taneesha. The world was vast, and Kovan's heart, wounded but not completely closed off, remained open to the potential of new connections and experiences.

POEM

Every day I went to school I hoped to catch a glance of you
All I want to do is talk to you; maybe take a little Ronda vow
After school I use to gaze into your eyes
And think way you don't realize that you're mine
I need you to survive! Not hypnotized, by your legs or thighs
Want to make love to your mind don't act as if it's a surprise
I finally got the opportunity to talk to you
But what did I do nothing, I was surprised by you
Spending time close together like we're supposed to do
The only image in my head is of me holding you
I beat myself up for days because I was too scary to say
That I think I love you, can I hug you
I'll place no one above you
Caramel skin, no coach I need you to win
I think I hear wedding bells; come on I can pretend
Where you go I want to roll, I need you to console
Not bold... just feeling old; my arms need you to hold

I'm cold and so alone, come and harm up my soul

Guess who? Kovan's on-again, off-again best friend Patrice reentered his life, but this time, she wasn't alone. Patrice had found herself a boyfriend and was expecting a baby. Unfortunately, their relationship was far from ideal. Kovan vividly remembered an incident when Patrice was at her boyfriend's house, and they got into a heated argument. Despite her pregnancy, he refused to take her home. In distress, Patrice reached out to Kovan for help.

Kovan immediately went to her boyfriend's house to escort Patrice safely home. It meant that he had to walk a considerable distance himself afterward, but he didn't hesitate. This was what best friends did for each other, and Kovan was determined to support Patrice through her difficulties.

During her pregnancy, Kovan would occasionally walk Patrice to the park, providing her with comfort and care. He would even go the extra mile and massage her feet, knowing that pregnancy could take a toll on a woman's body. These small acts of kindness were his way of showing support and being there for his friend during a challenging time.

Although Patrice's circumstances had changed, and their friendship had taken on new dynamics, Kovan remained steadfast in his role as a reliable and supportive companion. He was committed to being there for her as she navigated the joys and challenges of motherhood.

As the pattern went, the two were estranged once again. And as the pattern went, Kovan and Patrice reconciled once again sort of. Even though they were not on speaking terms at the time, Patrice's cousin reached out to Kovan from the hospital letting him know that Patrice had given birth to her son, Sion. Soon they managed to reconcile once again. Kovan was named Sion's unofficial godfather.

Following his graduation, Kovan faced the reality of life after high school. As his dreams of pursuing a football career didn't materialize, he decided it was time to find a job. However, before diving into the world of employment, he took a few months off to indulge in the freedom of doing nothing. Sleeping and waking up whenever he pleased gave him a sense of liberation, but soon the aimlessness started to weigh on him. He realized it was time to be proactive and take charge of his life.

With newfound motivation, Kovan secured a job at a retail store. He dedicated himself to this position for the next couple of years, gradually settling into a routine. It was during this time that he unexpectedly encountered Erin. They struck up a conversation as friends, catching up on the details of each other's lives that they had missed.

Erin, in Kovan's eyes, was someone who deviated from his usual type. Her personality wasn't something he would typically consider for a romantic relationship. Kovan questioned if she was this way in the past and did he just miss or overlook it. Despite the initial reservations, he was tired of being alone so he entertained her.

Kovan found himself enjoying their conversations and growing closer to Erin as they spent more time together. As Kovan embarked on this new chapter, he couldn't help but wonder if Erin could potentially be more than just a friend.

Despite Erin's affinity for profanity, marijuana, and a strong connection to rap culture, Kovan found himself drawn to her. He was willing to overlook these differences, driven by a sense of desperation to find companionship. Surprisingly, he noticed that those who surrounded him tended to adapt the way he carried himself.

CHAPTER 6:

DAYDREAMING

Their relationship continued to thrive, and they made the decision to take the next step and move in together. They found a small one-bedroom apartment, and Kovan was ecstatic to finally have his own space. Without much hesitation, he moved in a day earlier, even though he only had a single bag and a few other belongings. The excitement of independence and starting this new chapter overshadowed any concerns about material possessions.

The apartment became their sanctuary, a place where they could establish their own routines and build a life together. Although they came from different backgrounds and had contrasting interests, they managed to find common ground and navigate the challenges that arose.

Living together allowed Kovan to gain a deeper understanding of Erin's perspectives and experiences. It challenged his preconceived notions and provided an opportunity for growth and empathy. Their bond strengthened as they learned to appreciate each other's uniqueness and navigate the complexities of their relationship within the confines of their shared space.

As they settled into their new home, Kovan couldn't help but feel a sense of contentment and hope for the future. Despite the unconventional circumstances and the differences that once seemed daunting, he found solace in the connection they shared and the life they were building together. The small apartment held the promise of love, growth, and new beginnings.

Living independently brought a sense of freedom to Kovan's life, but he couldn't ignore the moral conflict that lingered in the back of his mind. He carried a feeling of guilt, knowing that his choices went against the values instilled by his grandmother, who had been a pillar of faith and spirituality in their family. This internal struggle made him hesitant to visit his grandmother, fearing the disappointment she might feel if she knew the truth about his living situation.

Despite this inner turmoil, Kovan's relationship with Erin continued to progress smoothly. She accepted and welcomed Patrice and her son Sion into their lives, and they would occasionally visit their apartment.

To address their transportation needs, they made the decision to purchase a car together. While Erin handled the payments, Kovan took responsibility for contributing his share by paying the rent. Their arrangement allowed them to share the car effectively, considering Kovan's overnight schedule.

The financial struggles they faced were not easily ignored, but their determination and teamwork helped them overcome these challenges. They managed to make ends meet and keep moving forward, clinging to the hope of a better future. Despite the external difficulties, they found comfort in their connection and the support they provided to each other.

In the midst of their financial and moral dilemmas, Kovan and Erin held onto the belief that they were on a path towards a brighter future. Their love and dedication to one another propelled them forward, despite the challenges they encountered along the way.

As Kovan and Erin continued their journey together, they decided to take a significant step in their commitment to each other by opening a joint bank account. It symbolized their growing partnership and their shared vision for a future together. Combining their financial resources was a practical decision that reflected their deepening bond.

They also embarked on a trip to North Carolina to visit Erin's mother. It was an opportunity for Kovan to meet her family and strengthen their connection. The visit allowed him to gain further insight into Erin's background and upbringing, fostering a deeper understanding of her as a person.

Daydreaming

During this time, Kovan's love for Erin grew even stronger, leading him to propose and ask her to be his partner for life. He saw her as the one he wanted to spend his future with, sharing dreams and building a life together. The engagement brought excitement and joy, solidifying their commitment to one another.

However, their happiness was soon marred by the reappearance of one of Erin's old friends, someone who exhibited behaviors that clashed with Kovan's values. This friend, who had previously embraced profanity, marijuana use, and a culture that didn't align with Kovan's preferences, resurfaced in Erin's life, bringing along negative influences.

This sudden return of Erin's old personality was a significant challenge for their relationship. Kovan found himself facing a situation where the person he had fallen in love with seemed to be changing, succumbing to negative influences that he didn't resonate with. It created tension and uncertainty within their once harmonious partnership.

Now, Kovan had to navigate the complexities of dealing with the reemergence of this friend and the impact it had on his relationship. He had to grapple with questions of trust, values, and whether the person he fell in love with still existed beneath the surface. The newfound difficulties threatened to disrupt the love and stability they had built together, testing the strength of their bond and their ability to overcome obstacles.

It was a challenging and uncertain time for Kovan and Erin, as they faced this unexpected turn in their relationship. The path ahead seemed unclear, and both of them would have to confront their own inner conflicts and make difficult decisions about the future of their partnership.

As days turned into nights, Kovan noticed a concerning change in Erin's behavior. She started staying out all night, leaving Kovan feeling abandoned and alone. Even after he finished his overnight shift at work, she would still be absent, leaving him to face the loneliness and uncertainty that crept into their shared apartment.

The evidence of Erin's lifestyle choices became increasingly apparent, with blunts left on the couch and other indications of her involvement with drugs. Kovan was disgusted by what he saw, feeling betrayed by the person he thought he knew and loved. It was a painful realization that their relationship had deteriorated to the point where they felt more like roommates than a couple.

During this tumultuous time, Kovan found comfort in the advice of his on-again, off-again best friend, Patrice. She had been there through thick and thin, witnessing the highs and lows of Kovan's

relationships. Patrice expressed her concerns about Erin, urging Kovan to leave her and find someone who would treat him better. However, Kovan's loyalty to Erin and the hope that things could improve kept him from heeding Patrice's warnings. He was determined to hold on, believing that there might still be a chance that the woman he fell in love with was still there.

One day, as Erin was about to head out, Kovan noticed a familiar face in the car that picked her up. It was an old teammate from high school, someone Kovan had once considered a friend. The sight struck him with a mix of confusion and frustration. Questions swirled in his mind. What was their connection? What was really happening behind the scenes?

The revelation intensified Kovan's doubts and further strained his already fragile trust in Erin. He couldn't shake off the feeling that something was deeply wrong. The distance between them grew, and their once-promising future together seemed to be slipping further out of reach.

In the midst of these difficult circumstances, Kovan was left with a difficult decision to make. Should he continue to hold onto the hope that things would improve, or should he confront the reality of their situation and consider whether it was time to let go? The uncertainty weighed heavily on his heart, as he grappled with his feelings of love, disappointment, and the fear of being alone.

The sight of Brian, Kovan's former offensive lineman from high school, being connected to Erin in some way heightened his suspicions and deepened his concerns. While they were not particularly close friends, their positions on the football team had brought them into contact and created a certain level of familiarity. However, what troubled Kovan the most was the knowledge that Brian and Erin had dated during their high school years.

The combination of their troubled relationship and the presence of Brian in Erin's life became a recipe for disaster in Kovan's mind. Doubts began to consume him, and he couldn't help but wonder if Erin had been unfaithful. He noticed a shift in their dynamics, a change in the way she behaved and carried herself, which only intensified his suspicions.

Though Kovan didn't possess concrete evidence of infidelity, the pieces of the puzzle seemed to fit together in a troubling way. He felt a sense of betrayal, questioning the trust he had placed in Erin and grappling with the idea that she might have cheated on him. The uncertainty and ambiguity of the situation added to his emotional turmoil.

As Kovan reflected on these mounting concerns, he couldn't help but feel a mix of anger, hurt, and disappointment. Their relationship, once filled with promise and love, had now become tainted by doubt and distrust. The foundation they had built together seemed to be crumbling, leaving Kovan to grapple with his emotions and contemplate the difficult decisions that lay ahead.

With each passing day, the weight of the situation became heavier on Kovan's shoulders, pushing him to confront the reality of his crumbling relationship and consider the difficult path forward. Although trying to put on a straight face.

POEM

There was a time when I thought I was done
The year of no fun back in 2001
I moved out on my own
Oh yeah I thought I was grown
When times got hard I had to show the ability to be strong
I had to save my pennies...So bad I was far from Fort Knocks

Rain On A Beautiful Day

I had to call Wells Fargo to see if I could go to Jack-in-the-box
I'm just saying man, dang
I don't know how much I can stand
To top it off my girlfriend's not by my side because she's playing
I tried to treat her special with no man to teach me how
I did my best but day by day I rarely seen her smile
A former love yeah man, I was high as a dove
But in return, all she did was sweep me under the rug
As time moved on, wow, things got worse
How would you feel to find your ring not in but under her purse?

POEM

I thought!
I needed you in my life to survive
I thought!
If I didn't have you I'll surely die
I thought!
You and I could share the American pie
I thought!
If times got tough, you would ride or die
I thought!
The words would hurt if you said goodbye
I thought wrong!
Now I'm gone because I'm done with your lies
You can go-head and cry and say I'm out of my mind
But in time you will find you were living a lie
So goodbye!

CHAPTER 7:

A TWIST OF FATE

Amidst the turmoil of his failing relationship with Erin and the unsettling suspicion of her potential infidelity, Kovan found comfort in an unexpected encounter at work. A girl named Taneesha, coincidentally sharing the same name as his high school sweetheart, entered his life.

Work-Taneesha, though she had been working at the same place for some time, had somehow gone unnoticed by Kovan until now. Intrigued by her presence, he asked her if her boyfriend would mind her having a male friend. She responded positively, revealing that she didn't have a boyfriend, and they exchanged numbers.

As Kovan and work-Taneesha began talking on a regular basis, a unique bond developed between them. Kovan found comfort in confiding his struggles, sharing the complexities of his failing relationship with Erin, and unburdening himself from the emotional weight he had been carrying.

Work-Taneesha, understanding and empathetic, became a sounding board for Kovan's frustrations, offering him a listening ear and providing a sense of understanding that he had been craving. Their conversations offered a respite from the turmoil he experienced with Erin, creating a sense of connection and camaraderie that Kovan hadn't felt in a long time.

With work-Taneesha by his side, Kovan began to see a glimmer of hope amidst the darkness. Her presence brought a renewed sense of optimism and the belief that there might be a chance for happiness beyond the confines of his current troubled relationship. Together, they navigated the complexities of his life.

Little did Kovan know that this unexpected connection with work-Taneesha would lead him on a path of self-discovery and open the doors to a new chapter in his life—one where he could find healing.

After months of struggling in his deteriorating relationship with Erin, Kovan finally made the difficult decision to heed the advice he had been receiving from both Patrice and work-Taneesha. With work-Taneesha's support and guidance, he gathered the courage to move his belongings out of the apartment while Erin was at work.

They worked together, packing up his belongings and making arrangements for his move. Throughout the process, Kovan couldn't help but notice the striking similarities between work-Taneesha and his first love, Taneesha, which only added to his growing sense of comfort and trust in her.

Meanwhile, Patrice's advice to leave Erin had been echoing in Kovan's mind for months. Looking back, he realized that the familiar connection he felt with work-Taneesha played a role in his decision to listen to her counsel. Both their names being Taneesha and sharing the same birthdate created a sense of comfort and resonance that influenced his trust in her guidance.

With his decision made, Kovan served Erin a thirty-day notice, signaling the end of their relationship. He made arrangements to move in with his grandmother, seeking the support and stability he longed for during this tumultuous time. The day of the move arrived, and as fate would have it, Brian, Erin's ex-boyfriend and Kovan's former teammate, was there to assist Erin with the stuff. Despite their shared history, there were no words exchanged between Kovan and Brian. They simply walked past each other, acknowledging the chapter they had both played in Erin's life.

In the aftermath, Kovan's interactions with Erin and Brian became infrequent, and he eventually heard through the grapevine that they had married and started a family. Though the news carried a bittersweet tinge, Kovan hoped to embark on a new chapter in his life, guided by the support and connection he had found with work-Taneesha.

A Twist Of Fate

In the wake of the painful breakup with Erin, Kovan found himself in a state of emotional turmoil. The fragments of his heart seemed irreparably shattered, and he couldn't help but drive past their old apartment, lost in bittersweet memories that stung with each passing moment. The weight of the breakup was so heavy that it consumed him, and he often found himself staring into the mirror, tears streaming down his face, questioning why things had to end and why Erin had changed.

Miserable became Kovan's constant companion, his heartache radiating through every fiber of his being. The absence of Erin's presence left him feeling empty and lost. His coworkers at work could sense his despair, recognizing that something was amiss, but he struggled to open up about his pain. Whenever he attempted to speak about it, the tears threatened to overwhelm him, rendering him speechless. He did his best to maintain a focus at work, but the weight of his sorrow made it increasingly difficult to focus on his tasks.

POEM

You know they say that opposites attack
That can't be true because in my life, it's just not a fact
I feel I'm a good person, it can't be me
Every time I think I've found love I get kicked down by Bruce Lee
It's crazy playing tug-of-war mental
Mind telling you leave, heart saying just stay
I'm strong so I got to find another place to lay
Forget it; I'm give up on love, it's going straight to the trash
I figured it out, well in my case it just doesn't last
As I look back, I see that it went by real fast
It's a given, sooner or later life's' going to put you on blast
You see some form of love everywhere you go
Why then did I have to get hit by cupid's toxic bow?

POEM

They call it a tragedy
They say I'm not living in true reality
If thinking of her makes me happy
Why yall mad at me

Rain On A Beautiful Day

They say it's sad to see a real life true tragedy
Call her your majesty cause she rules inside of me
Yall say I'm scared to see that me and her weren't mint to be
It's like yall trying to turn my best friend to my enemy
Thought yall were a friend to me
Acting more like a frenemy
Wouldn't yall act more like yall ken to me
And tell me that it's mint to be
I'm wasting my time always thinking about you
I don't know why my skies are not blue
Through this window
I'm starting to think that maybe you're truly done with me
I'm starting to see that maybe we were never mint to be
It's starting to sink losing every single memory
I'm thinking we peaked and your love wasn't my destiny
Sure I'll start over
Done with this rollercoaster
Walk past like I don't know her to show her my heart is sober
Inside I want to expose her
Let the world see her a bit closer
That she aint all that she seems she's ready to reek your dreams

Transitioning from living independently to moving in with his grandmother had taken a toll on Kovan's emotional well-being. The stark contrast between the freedom he once enjoyed and the new arrangement intensified his unrealistic yearning to return to his old apartment. Every day felt like a battle as Kovan grappled with the aftermath of the breakup.

The deep longing to reclaim what was lost, coupled with the emotional strain he endured, tested his resilience. Despite the overwhelming sadness, he knew deep down that he had made the right decision by leaving Erin. It was in these moments of introspection that he began to find strength and started to envision a brighter future, one where his heart would heal and love would find its way back into his life.

Little did Kovan know that the journey he was embarking upon would lead him to discover new paths, unexpected connections, and ultimately, the healing he desperately sought. With time, patience, and the support of loved ones, he would begin to rebuild his life and uncover a renewed sense of purpose and happiness.

In the midst of Kovan's heartache, his attention naturally turned to work-Taneesha, the woman who had been a supportive friend during his difficult times. They had been spending more time together, getting to know each other on a deeper level. As their bond grew stronger, Kovan felt the urge to take their relationship to the next level and officially become a couple.

One day, while they were on the phone, Kovan mustered the courage to ask work-Taneesha out, hoping for a positive response. However, to his surprise and disappointment, she expressed a desire to remain friends. Kovan knew deep down that he couldn't settle for just being friends, as his heart longed for a romantic connection. It was a difficult realization, but he made the choice to speak his truth.

Sadly, that conversation marked the last time Kovan and work-Taneesha ever spoke. Unbeknownst to him, she had recently ended a relationship with the security guard at their workplace. It was during Kovan's journey to work one fateful night that he witnessed an unexpected sight—he saw work-Taneesha embracing her ex-boyfriend. Her attempt to avoid his gaze by moving to the opposite side of the street only confirmed Kovan's suspicion that their connection had come to an end.

POEM

I can take you from your man if you want to leave
No really girl, sincerely girl come fly away with me
I'll capture all your dreams and serve it to you on the sea
This isn't a supplication but here is where you ought to be
A shrewd man, not rude man… protecting you
Rendering things, I'll make you sing…do what it do
This prevalent world is just a danger to my girl
Exasperating your man…he knows the truth girl
No enmities in my heart, because I care for you girl
I was there from the start, you just didn't see me girl
Stood in the shadows just hoping and praying that you'll see
But I'm out now…scream out loud leave with me

After that encounter, work-Taneesha moved on to a better job, disappearing from Kovan's life completely. They never crossed paths again, and the memories of their friendship and the unrequited feelings Kovan had for her became fragments of a chapter that had reached its conclusion. Though he carried the scars of past heartaches, Kovan knew he had to continue forward, seeking a love that would be reciprocated and nurtured.

Little did he know that the universe had other plans in store for him. With each passing day, Kovan would learn and grow, becoming wiser and more resilient. He would soon realize that true love, genuine connections, and happiness were waiting for him in unexpected places, ready to heal his heart and guide him towards a brighter future.

Kovan couldn't help but entertain a lingering thought in his mind: was work-Taneesha sent into his life for a specific purpose? The timing of her arrival and subsequent departure seemed too coincidental to ignore. Perhaps, he pondered, she was a guiding force meant to lead him away from the toxic relationship with Erin. The way she appeared and then disappeared, leaving no trace behind, added to the mystery.

In retrospect, Kovan acknowledged that work-Taneesha's presence had a profound impact on his life. Without her, he might have remained stuck in a relationship that brought him nothing but misery. He admitted that he hadn't been willing to listen to the advice of others, but work-Taneesha's intervention had somehow reached him in a way no one else could. It was as if she had a hidden purpose, a mission to help him break free from the shackles of his unhappiness. Kovan would forever be grateful for the role she played in his journey, even if the mystery of her true identity remained unresolved.

A Twist Of Fate

POEM

There was a girl who was there in my life for a minute
She disappeared like the switch of a light need some healing
Helped me move on like a tricycle bike UHaul billing
But now she's done now I'm trapped in plain sight call me Griffin
Come on baby what you gonna do
No more to say girl it's up to you
Cards on the table and don't want to loss
Tell me that you want go
Tell me that you want stay
Tell me that you want roll
Baby I will find a place
She helped me move on she helped me stay hard
I'm all in it
I turned and she's gone reflection is wrong
Are we finished
She throw me a bone then left me alone
Like old lemons
I'm writing this poem just wishing I'm wrong
Come on baby what you gonna do
No more to say girl it's up to you
Cards on the table and don't want to loss
Losing you
Tell me that you want go
Tell me that you want stay
Tell me that you want roll
Baby I will find a place

POEM

There's only a few who I let get as close as you
Now that you're gone, what in the world am I supposed to do?
Who would've known the next day I'd feel so alone
Look at the clock, so slow now that my buddy is gone
You use to tell me everything from four to six
You know I'm listening, stir me up because I'm all in the mix
Remember I asked you to promise not to give up on love
Well right now, I need you to promise that you'll send me a sub
What can I say, you spoiled me; I just need someone to talk to

Rain On A Beautiful Day

I know there are others around, but none are like you
There like un-trained dogs, their quick to bite you
You turn your back to do good and their quit to spite you
Its official I miss you
Your friendship is essential
It's vital, your title
When it comes to friends your than idol
Despite all the pain
You left me with no disdain
I'll maintain, I'll reframe to blame you for the rain

CHAPTER 8:

CLOSE STRANGER

As Kovan's world was shifting and evolving, he found solace and support from his most common source—his long-time friend, Patrice. Through the ups and downs, she had remained a constant presence, never wavering in her loyalty and care for him. Their bond grew stronger, and Kovan began to see Patrice in a different light. He realized the depth of their connection and the unwavering support she had always offered.

In moments of vulnerability, Kovan always found himself turning to Patrice for comfort and understanding. They started to embark on late-night drives to random residential neighborhoods, where they would simply talk and confide in one another. These intimate conversations brought them closer, and Kovan began to see the beauty and strength within Patrice that he had overlooked before.

It was during one of these moments, in a serene park setting, that Kovan's feelings for Patrice reached a tipping point. As their eyes met, he could sense the anticipation and nervousness in the air. Unable to resist the magnetic pull between them, he gently pulled her closer and kissed her. The moment was priceless for Patrice, etched in her memories. Patrice's reaction was a mix of surprise, joy, and vulnerability, her hands moving slowly over her cheeks, overwhelmed by the newfound connection they shared.

From that moment on, Kovan realized that his feelings for Patrice had grown beyond friendship. He cherished her presence in his life and expressed his deep appreciation for her unwavering support. With his heart on his sleeve, he asked Patrice to be his girlfriend, solidifying their romantic bond.

Their journey from friends to lovers had begun, and Kovan couldn't be happier. He recognized the incredible person Patrice was and how lucky he was to have her by his side. Their friendship had served as a strong foundation for their blossoming romance, and their connection only grew stronger with each passing day.

Together, they embarked on a new chapter of their lives, filled with love, understanding, and unwavering support for one another. Kovan knew that he had finally found someone who would always be there for him, just as Patrice had been all along.

POEM

Sometimes I sit around and think wow
We've been friends for eight years
Through the good times and even a few tears
You continue to stand tall over all my peers
With you by my side, I can't go wrong
With you by my side, I will stay strong
With you by my side, the days don't seem long
Can you stay by my side, so I won't feel weak to the bone?
Former females seem to always bail
But there's one female that I'll never fail
You know it's you
Whenever I'm down and out, I look to you
To clear my gray skies and turn them blue
You always know just what to say
Through my trials and tribulations, you brighten my day
I know I haven't been the most reliable (god) father
But as he gets older, I'll make sure no one bothers
Sion, that is, I still can't believe you had a kid
Created by you and I, sometimes I wish we did
This is a dangerous time we soon will find
That it's hard to go back once you've crossed the line
From here on out, I'll try not to act like a jerk
This pen just won't stop, man I have to get back to work
So I'll leave you with this and try not to cross the line
Because a beautiful, true friend is always hard to find

As Kovan and Patrice embarked on their romantic journey, they faced their fair share of challenges. While their relationship was strong, there were certain differences and issues they had to navigate.

One significant difference between them was their outlook on life. Patrice had a tendency to be idealistic, often drawing inspiration from movies and envisioning a reality that mirrored the cinematic world. Kovan, on the other hand, took a more grounded approach and reminded her that movies were fictional creations, scripted and acted out for entertainment purposes. He tried to bring a sense of realism into their discussions, encouraging her to separate fantasy from reality.

Another obstacle arose when Kovan discovered that Patrice had taken up smoking. Concerned for her health and well-being, he made it clear that he couldn't continue in a relationship where one partner was engaging in a habit that posed significant risks. He urged Patrice to give up smoking, emphasizing the importance of prioritizing their long-term health and happiness.

Patrice assured Kovan that she would quit smoking, understanding the gravity of his concerns. However, Kovan soon realized that her resolve was tested when her mother, who was still a smoker, would ask her for cigarettes. This created tension and trust issues within their relationship, as Kovan questioned whether Patrice was truly committed to quitting.

Despite these challenges, Kovan and Patrice persevered. They engaged in open and honest conversations about their differences and concerns, striving to find common ground and maintain a healthy relationship. Patrice made efforts to break free from the influence of smoking. Their love and determination to make things work allowed them to navigate these hurdles together. It was a constant journey of understanding, compromise, and growth. They learned to appreciate each other's perspectives while also working on aligning their values and priorities.

Through it all, Kovan remained steadfast in his commitment to Patrice, recognizing that no relationship is perfect and that challenges are opportunities for growth. He believed in the potential of their love and was willing to support Patrice through her struggles, hoping that she would ultimately choose a healthier path for herself and their future together.

As Kovan delved deeper into his relationship with Patrice, he discovered that she had a penchant for creating special moments and celebrating every milestone. While this trait both fascinated and overwhelmed him, he wanted to show his love and support for her in a way that was meaningful to both of them.

One particular tradition that Patrice enjoyed was collecting a section from the Sunday newspaper featuring two cartoon characters with love-based messages. However, one day, she expressed that it was pointless for her to continue collecting them since he didn't show much interest.

Seeing how hurt Patrice was by this decision, Kovan decided to take matters into his own hands. He went on a secret mission to collect those newspaper sections for her. Every Sunday after work, he would make a special trip to the store, purchase the newspaper, and carefully cut out the beloved cartoon section that held sentimental value for Patrice.

Week after week, Kovan diligently stored these cut-outs, forming a collection that would later become a heartfelt gift. For two to three months, he silently gathered the cartoon sections, cherishing the opportunity to make Patrice happy.

Finally, the day arrived when Kovan was ready to reveal his surprise. He presented Patrice with the carefully collected collection of love-themed cartoon cut-outs. As she opened the gift, her excitement and joy filled the room, radiating a warmth that touched Kovan's heart. He had succeeded in making her happy, and that brought him immense satisfaction and fulfillment.

But Kovan didn't stop there. Among the amassed collection, he had created his own personalized cartoon message. In the final cut-out, one of the characters held a bunch of cut-outs behind his back, symbolizing the effort and love Kovan had poured into this endeavor.

The moment was magical as Patrice realized the extent of Kovan's devotion and thoughtfulness. It reinforced the depth of their connection and served as a reminder that love can be expressed in the simplest, yet most meaningful gestures.

From that day forward, the collection of love-themed cartoon cut-outs held an even greater significance for Patrice and Kovan. It became a testament to their bond, a symbol of the effort and affection they shared.

Through this heartfelt gesture, Kovan showed Patrice that he not only understood her quirks and desires but also wholeheartedly supported and embraced them. It was a small but powerful gesture that solidified their love and fostered a sense of deep appreciation between them.

CHAPTER 9:

RAIN ON A BEAUTIFUL DAY

One day, just out of the blue, Kovan, before taking Patrice her lunch for work, decided to stop by his ex-girlfriend Taneesha's home. Even with the intention of reconnecting as friends, this decision brought unexpected surprises. As he arrived on her familiar street, he noticed her two younger brothers playing in front of the house. Their excited voices called out his name, urging him to come inside and see their mom.

Curiosity piqued, Kovan entered the house, where he was warmly greeted by Taneesha's parents. They were genuinely delighted to see him, reminiscing about old times and expressing their fondness for him. In that moment, Kovan couldn't help but feel a sense of nostalgia and curiosity about Taneesha's life.

Taneesha was at home, but to his surprise, Taneesha's mother, Theresea, suggested calling her at work and putting her on speakerphone. Though Kovan had only intended to catch up with her at a later time, he found himself thrust into a conversation with his ex-girlfriend, unexpectedly hearing her voice after all these years. As soon as he heard her voice, he knew he was in terrible trouble.

The conversation between Kovan and Taneesha was a mix of awkwardness, nostalgia, and curiosity. They exchanged brief updates on their lives, sharing snippets of their experiences since their high school days. It was clear that time had brought changes and new directions for both of them.

As the call concluded, Kovan realized that his impromptu visit had stirred up emotions within him. He questioned the motives behind his desire to reconnect with Taneesha and whether it was a wise decision to go back into the past. It made him ponder the significance of the present and the future he was building with Patrice.

Leaving Taneesha's home that day, Kovan felt a whirlwind of thoughts and emotions. It served as a reminder that even the simplest of actions can have unexpected consequences and can unearth emotions and memories that were buried in the past.

Reflecting on the encounter, Kovan realized the importance of focusing on the present and cherishing the relationship he had with Patrice. It was a wake-up call that reminded him of the depth of his connection with Patrice and the need to nurture and appreciate the love they shared.

From that moment forward, Kovan made a conscious effort to invest his energy and attention into his current relationship with Patrice. He recognized the value of the present and the future they were building together, vowing to leave the past where it belonged and embrace the love and connection he had with Patrice wholeheartedly.

But Kovan couldn't shake the emotions he felt after hearing Taneesha's voice on the phone, how the rush of emotions and memories flooded back, how it caught him off guard.

The encounter with Taneesha left Kovan in a state of turmoil. When he arrived at Patrice's workplace to drop off her lunch, he couldn't shake off the awkwardness that had consumed him. Conflicting thoughts swirled in his mind, questioning the possibility of being in love with two people and whether his reawakened feelings for Taneesha would jeopardize his relationship with Patrice. Uncertainty loomed over him as he grappled with his emotions.

Attempting to find some semblance of focus, Kovan went to work that night, but his mind was far from the tasks at hand. Lost in contemplation, he was suddenly interrupted by an announcement over the loudspeaker, informing him that he had a phone call. Intrigued and curious about who would be calling him at work, as it was a rare occurrence, mostly limited to requests from Kevin, who needed permission to access his locked room back home. The unexpected phone call added an element of intrigue to an already tumultuous day.

With a mix of anticipation and trepidation, Kovan embarked on this unexpected conversation, unsure of what awaited him on the other end of the line. Little did he know that this phone call would serve as a turning point in his journey, offering him a chance to confront his emotions, make decisions, and ultimately shape the course of his future.

As Kovan reached the phone, his heart skipped a beat when he heard Taneesha's voice on the other end. Instantly, a flood of memories rushed back, transporting him to a time when they would spend countless hours talking on the phone, sharing their deepest thoughts and dreams. The nostalgia enveloped him, tugging at his heartstrings.

At that moment, Kovan and Taneesha made a spontaneous decision to meet for breakfast, unable to resist the pull of their shared history. As Kovan arrived to pick her up, he couldn't help but be captivated by her radiant beauty. Yet, he also felt a sense of responsibility, a reminder that he was currently in a committed relationship with Patrice. He had to tread carefully, reminding himself to keep his emotions in check.

Over breakfast, they embarked on a journey down memory lane, relishing in the opportunity to catch up and reminisce about their past. As they delved into their shared experiences, a sense of familiarity and comfort settled between them. However, amidst the laughter and shared stories, an unexpected moment of vulnerability unfolded.

A single tear rolled down Taneesha's cheek, speaking volumes about the emotions that lay dormant within her. In that instant, the weight of their history and the complexities of their current circumstances became evident. Kovan's own eyes welled up with tears, mirroring the depth of their unspoken connection.

Aware that their emotions were spiraling and that they needed space to process their feelings, they mutually decided to leave the breakfast place. It was a bittersweet moment, marked by the undeniable chemistry and the realization that they had to confront the complicated reality they found themselves in.

In the days that followed, Kovan noticed the lingering sense of distance he felt with Patrice. Though physically present, his mind was preoccupied with thoughts of Taneesha. The guilt of emotional infidelity weighed heavily on him, and he knew he needed to confront the truth and make a difficult decision.

Summoning the courage to have an honest conversation, Kovan expressed to Taneesha that it was only fair for him to remain committed to Patrice. While she didn't agree with his choice, Taneesha understood the complexity of the situation. The heartbreak in her voice resonated with Kovan, and he couldn't help but feel a sense of devastation himself.

Struggling to reconcile his feelings, Kovan recognized that his relationship with Patrice had started as a rebound. He had sought comfort and companionship in her during a time of emotional turmoil, but it became clear that he wasn't truly in love with her. It was a painful realization, and he deeply regretted the hurt he had caused.

Despite his efforts to salvage their relationship, Kovan couldn't deny the growing disconnect between him and Patrice. Every little thing Patrice did got on Kovan's nerves. The once vibrant flame that had ignited between them had dimmed, unable to withstand the weight of unresolved emotions and unrequited love. It was a difficult admission, but Kovan knew that he had to be honest with himself.

Reflecting on the events that had led him to Patrice, the failed friendships, and the unresolved feelings for Taneesha, Kovan understood that he had sought comfort in the person who had been there for him. Patrice had been his rock, his support, but their connection was built on a foundation of unhealed wounds and unfulfilled desires.

As Kovan came to terms with his own truth, he knew that he needed to find the strength to end things with Patrice. It was a painful decision, one that would undoubtedly bring heartache and disappointment. However, he couldn't deny the necessity of seeking true happiness and authentic love, even if it meant facing the consequences of his actions.

Feeling the weight of his decision, Kovan mustered the courage to visit Patrice and address the situation head-on. As he arrived at her home, he took a deep breath and began to speak, admitting that he may have jumped into the relationship too fast. He expressed his belief that they needed some time apart.

Patrice, taken aback by his sudden revelation, confessed that she hadn't perceived any significant issues in their relationship. She questioned his decision, seeking answers and clarity. Kovan knew that revealing the true reason behind his choice was not an option, for the sake of both his and Taneesha's safety.

Patrice wanted this relationship for years. She felt that Taneesha was the one that stood in her way in the past. So to confess that Tanessha was the reason they were breaking up would have been dangerous in Kovan's eyes. Choosing his words carefully, Kovan assured Patrice that it wasn't her fault, emphasizing that he needed to focus on himself and find his own path. He acknowledged their shared struggles but stressed that it wasn't the reason why. Though it pained him to deceive her, Kovan knew that this was the only way.

POEM

How are you doing today
I have a lot to say but…
Not going to be on my way cause…
I just can't see your face.. And…
When I left you' you were lonely
Screaming I need someone to hold me
What if your not doing fine
What if things aren't alright
What if you gave up the fight
Girl I know I left you lonely
Screaming I need someone to hold me
I see the tears in your eyes but this is goodbye
How are you doing today
I got a lot to say but…

Rain On A Beautiful Day

Not going to be on my way cause…
I just can't see your face.. And
When I left you we were homies
Would pillow talk until the morning
What if your not doing fine
What if things aren't alright
That's what I got on my mind
Girl I know you left you lonely
Screaming I need someone to hold
I see the tears in your eyes but this is goodbye
Girl I know you left you lonely
Screaming I need someone to hold
I see the tears in your eyes
Girl I know you left you lonely
Screaming I need someone to hold
I see the tears in your eyes but this is goodbye
I've been meaning to tell you that I'm sorry
I've been meaning to tell you I was wrong
I was wrong by the things I said to you
I was wrong by the things I said I'd do
I was wrong when I said I'm over you

With a heavy heart, Kovan left Patrice that night and headed to work, his mind consumed by conflicting emotions. In the solitude of his workplace, he reached out to Taneesha, recounting the events and seeking solace in their shared understanding. As they conversed, a sense of calm washed over them, providing a brief respite from the chaos of their intertwined lives.

The next morning, as Kovan prepared to go home, his phone rang. It was Patrice, reaching out to him, yearning for closure and perhaps one last chance to salvage their relationship. Uncertain about what awaited him, Kovan agreed to stop by before returning home, knowing that this encounter would be an emotional and potentially pivotal moment for both of them.

As Patrice entered the car, the weight of their emotions hung heavily in the air. She desperately sought a glimmer of hope, hoping to salvage their relationship. Kovan, seeing her pain, almost gave in to a moment of weakness and continued the relationship. But his heart cried out to him screaming no! So he stood strong and restated that he jumped into their relationship too soon after his breakout. Her tears mirrored Kovan's own as they confronted the painful reality that their journey together had reached its end. The depth of their shared history and friendship only intensified their heartbreak, as they knew that the bonds they once cherished were irreparably broken.

As the car became a sanctuary for their shared grief, they both acknowledged the finality of their separation. In a symbolic gesture of closure, Patrice returned every memento and token of affection Kovan had given her over the course of their relationship, including the cartoon cut-outs. With each item exchanged, their bond fractured further, sealing the fate of their eight-year friendship.

From that poignant day forward, their paths never crossed again, and communication between them ceased entirely. The echoes of their laughter, inside jokes, and shared memories became distant whispers as they embarked on separate journeys, forever severed from the once unbreakable bond they had shared for nine years.

POEM

I had a best friend whose bond I thought would never end
Until we broke the unwritten rule, by commending an ultimate sin
We were unstoppable for eight years through all the boos and cheers
Through my toughest times, she was there by my side
She would banish my fears and even comfort me in tears
But 2004 really opened the door
It turned out to be the beginning of the end because sin crept in
Saying, their friendship's too pure; false love should kill that for sure
While confessing my love, one no could interrupt
But the responses I got were, "Man, you sure messed up"
I didn't listen because it just felt right
No more Miss Phillips; I'll change her last name to White
You'll never know if your love is real until it's tested with time
If your love stands tall, then you'll be just fine
I can't say the same thing happened with mine
If it did then, I wouldn't be writing this rhyme
June 14th, 2004, was my defining test of time
That's when I saw my ex Taneesha in a very long time

Rain On A Beautiful Day

"We can be friends" is what was on my mind
All that was lost, as soon as I looked in her eyes
I'm lying; I was gone the night before when I first heard her voice
Soon after I knew, she was my number one choice
From that point on, I knew I wasn't like the average man
They said, "Player, you've got, not one but two females wanting to
hold your hand
You're dealing with feelings here; most men just wouldn't
understand
It's your move Kovan; come on; which way's your heart going to
land
Either way I go, the mess is going to hit the fan
Someone's heart torn to pieces, that's what I can't stand,
So I let my heart do all the talking; my mind stayed out the way
My heart belonged to Taneesha; it was just on layaway
Left on the shelf too long, I began to collect dust
My first love is back; she's the one my heart trusts
Without prolonging the pain, I had to let Patrice go
My emotions filled with sorrow, as I fell to one knee
I'm losing my godson, god spelled with a lowercase 'g'
First came Patrice, now Leon I can't even see
Sometimes I wonder does he ever think about me
A positive role model is what I was trying to be
To Sion my little man, a good man he'll be
He needs a male role model that's truly the key
I pray for him every day because most likely that male won't be me
I miss you
Mother and Son

POEM

Was missing you then
still missing you now
Don't know whom I'm missing more
girl is it you or your child
I'm missing your smile
I'm missing yelling out loud
You're my best friend
Who knew that our friendship would end?
Why did we give in? A part of me is missing again

Rain On A Beautiful Day

Girl can you forgive
Say yes because I'm struggling to live
I'm missing little man
Lady please understand
There's nothing that I miss more than simply holding his hand
It seems that I'm banned...blow up
Now there's my heart going to land
I'm stuck in the sand
Please save me when I reach out my hand
Just give me a chance
I need it so my heart could advance

CHAPTER 10:

THE PLAN ALL ALONG

Kovan and Taneesha, having weathered the storm of their complicated history, continued to navigate the uncertainties and complexities of their evolving relationship. Their shared experiences and newfound commitment to each other gave them the strength to face the future together, one step at a time.

As Kovan reflected on the painful aftermath of his decision, a deep sense of guilt and remorse washed over him. He couldn't shake the feeling that Patrice had been caught in the crossfire of his emotional journey, a casualty of his pursuit of happiness and peace of mind. Despite knowing that breaking up was the right choice for his well-being, the weight of his actions bore heavily on his conscience.

In the midst of his internal struggle, Kovan couldn't help but draw parallels between the strained relationships he and Taneesha had with their respective godchildren. It was as if the universe had orchestrated a series of separations, cutting ties that might have entangled their lives further. While he couldn't help but wonder if these separations were a sign, a means of freeing them from the potential burdens and complications that children could bring, he couldn't dismiss the bittersweet emotions that accompanied such thoughts.

Amidst the introspection, Kovan held onto the hope that both Patrice and Sion would find happiness in their own paths. He wished them well, fervently praying that their journeys would lead them to fulfilling lives and the love they deserved. Yet, he knew that he had to prioritize his own healing and newfound love with Taneesha, focusing on building a future together unencumbered by past regrets and what-ifs.

POEM

A little boy's out in the world that was as close as can be
I loved him since day one; he was like a son to me
He was my godson, was it official? No
But he made me feel like a father; boy I miss him so
You know there are some days when I start to feel real low
It's starting to look gray because he's not there to make that part of
me glow
I really doubt that Leon will ever come back into my life
You see his mom and I are no longer together, and she wanted to
become my wife
So I will just continue to pray and wish for the best
Because deep in my heart I know I was head and shoulders above
the rest
It seems no one in my life really understands
How could they? It's a story in my life
It's not fair to try and put it in their hands
I tend to hear...don't worry about it or let it go
I try to wrap my brain around it, but my heart immediately says no
I've been given different keys to move on and open different doors
But that's not easy to do when it comes to someone you have love
for
So much time spent wondering…what Leon would think of me now.
Would he walk right by, frown, would he even notice my smile?
I can't help thinking how much I could be letting him down
If he remembers, would he grow up to hate me?
Or be sarcastic and go ahead and thank me
For not being there in his times of need
When he was looking for someone who had the quality to lead
For him not to remember me; that's one of my biggest fears
It would be all my fault though, no need to comfort my tears

With a mix of gratitude and trepidation, Kovan embraced the notion that their paths had aligned for a reason. The challenges they faced, the losses they endured, and the sacrifices they made had shaped their bond and allowed them to find solace in each other's arms. They vowed to cherish their newfound love and forge ahead, holding onto the hope that their shared journey would be one of growth, understanding, and unyielding love.

As Kovan and Taneesha embarked on this new chapter of their lives, the decision to purchase a home symbolized their commitment and shared vision for the future. Settling in Antelope Valley brought a sense of stability and the opportunity to create a place of their own, filled with love, laughter, and the promise of a bright future together.

The process of turning their house into a home was a labor of love. They spent time arranging furniture and infusing the space with their unique personalities and shared memories. Each room became a reflection of their journey, with photographs capturing their most cherished moments adorning the walls. The house quickly transformed into a sanctuary, a haven where their love and dreams could flourish.

As they settled into their new home, Kovan and Taneesha continued to explore the depths of their relationship, nurturing their connection and growing together as a couple. They discovered new shared interests, embarked on adventures, and supported each other's personal aspirations. With open hearts and unwavering commitment, they navigated the joys and challenges that life brought their way.

Surrounded by the beauty of their love, Kovan and Taneesha found comfort in knowing that they had finally found their way back into each other's arms. Their journey, filled with twists and turns, had led them to this point of blissful contentment. Together, they revealed the blessings of a love that was true, profound, and destined to withstand the tests of time.

POEM

When you weren't in my life, girl, I was feeling real bad
Was left in the cold, girl, I was feeling real sad
You sheltered me from the breeze, now I'm no longer mad, only
glad
To have you in my life, to make you my wife
Finally getting it right, girl, every day, every night
Yeah, girl, I'm willing to fight, girl, what an eye-catching light

Rain On A Beautiful Day

Blinding people with our love, cause we're shining so bright
Blinding people with our love, baby, you're out of sight
It's that funny feeling you get every time you see her
It warms you up inside every time she's near
When you look in her eyes, it's like you can't even speak
You'll tell her all your secrets, won't even care if it leaks
Twenty-four hours a day, this girl stays on your mind
You found a diamond in the rough; man, she sure is fine
My one and only wish was to make you mine
To the man that let you pass, I swear my must be blind
I'm staring at trees
Hoping, begging please
Got me on my knees for a squeeze
Give me what I need
It's you, what more to do
Keep a hold on what's true
It's new, only we knew
That this thing is beautiful
Our love, high as a dove
Our feet will never touch down
Your sound, don't beat around
Cause true love is what we've found
I'm down to be with you
Tell me what you want to do
If you're through, then I'm through
Cause I can't breathe without you

As they celebrated their first wedding anniversary in their cozy Antelope Valley home, Kovan and Taneesha looked back on their individual paths, the tumultuous relationships they had overcome, and the transformative power of love. Grateful for the lessons learned and the strength they had gained.

In the warm embrace of their new home, Kovan and Taneesha found the peace and fulfillment they had longed for. Their love story, born out of heartbreak and resilience, had blossomed into something extraordinary—a testament to the resilience of the human spirit and the enduring power of love to heal, restore, and create a life worth living.

The Plan All Along

The long commute had initially posed a challenge for Kovan and Taneesha as they navigated the daily journey to their respective workplaces. However, their unwavering commitment to each other and their shared goals kept them motivated to find a better solution. Still, they relished the moments spent carpooling, using the time to connect, share stories. The road became a canvas for their dreams, a space where they could plan and envision their future.

In their determination to create a more balanced and efficient routine, Kovan and Taneesha began exploring job opportunities closer to their new home in Antelope Valley. They sought out positions that would not only minimize their commuting time but also provide them with fulfilling careers.

Taneesha's efforts bore fruit as she secured a job closer to their home. The new chapter in her professional life brought a sense of relief and a renewed enthusiasm for their future together. Kovan was still burdened by long hours spent on the road, postponing the extra time they hoped to have to invest in their relationship and personal pursuits.

Even though only Taneesha had a shorter commute, their lives fell into a rhythm that allowed them to thrive. As they settled into their new routine, Kovan and Taneesha experienced a sense of harmony and balance in their lives. The challenges they had faced early on had only strengthened their bond and taught them the importance of adaptability and perseverance.

The decision to move had proven to be a turning point in their journey. It had brought them closer physically, emotionally, and spiritually, setting the stage for a future filled with love, fulfillment, and the shared joys of building a life together in their cherished home.

POEM

I want to take this time to tell you how much your love means to me
Without you, my life is empty, like my lungs with no air to breathe
What I'm trying to say is, you give me life, a beautiful reason to live
My heart, body, and soul to you is what I'll give
All those years you were gone, I knew there was something I lacked

Rain On A Beautiful Day

But I'm totally complete now because I got my baby back
I always felt your ten-year plan just wasn't meant to be
Why? Because I just can't wait ten years for you to marry me
Man, those beautiful eyes I thought I'd never see
It looks more vibrant and green now that you're a part of my family
tree
Can I hold you forever and never let you go?
Can I kiss you softly, to let your heart know?
I'm here for you and only you, I want to make your heart glow
A bright red, blinding everyone with our love
Not from this earth, you were sent from up above
If you were a show, you'd be on primetime
I'll never disgrace you because you're way more than a dime
You're an artist everyone wants to feature
I'll always protect our love from any man, woman, or creature
Can it get any better than this?
The answer is no, because I'm in pure bliss
It's been about five years, and every single day I've missed
Your love, your hug, down to the simplest kiss
You were an old flame that was lost overnight
The only way we'll end this time is if I lose the fight
Just being around you drives me crazy
I think about you all day long
And I'll admit, it makes me a little bit lazy
As time passed on, I thought I had finally let you go
But as soon as I heard your voice, my heart and mind told me no
It must be true love for me to hold on after all these years
It will be easy to treat you right because without you, it was hard for
me to stop the tears
You're finally back in my life, and I'm filled with so much joy
It's like the expression on a kid's face when they receive their brand
new toy

CHAPTER 11:

WINDY ROAD

One day while driving home from work, Kovan's exhaustion caught up with him, causing him to doze off behind the wheel on the freeway. The screeching sound of his car scraping against the guardrail jolted him awake, narrowly avoiding a potentially disastrous accident. This wasn't the first time such an incident had occurred, as Kovan had been struggling with the exhausting daily commute to and from work for quite some time.

On another occasion, Kovan had fallen asleep while driving to work and was pulled over by a police officer for speeding. The officer questioned why he didn't pull over when the lights were activated, and Kovan honestly admitted that he was relieved to be stopped because he had actually fallen asleep at the wheel. This incident added to his growing concerns about his safety and the safety of others on the road.

Feeling desperate to move closer to home and put an end to these dangerous situations, Kovan began exploring the possibility of transferring to a location nearer to his residence. However, in his eagerness to speed up the process, he reached out to the other store before discussing it with his current one. This approach didn't sit well with either store, leading to the denial of the transfer request.

Frustrated with his job and still fearing the potential consequences of falling asleep while driving, Kovan persisted in his pursuit of a transfer closer to home. He didn't want to leave the company where he had been a loyal employee for six years, preferring to stay within the familiar work environment. However, with the implementation of a new policy under the new governor, all employees were mandated to take their lunch breaks before their fifth hour of work. The policy allowed for two chances, with the first being a verbal warning and the second a written warning. Unfortunately, Kovan received two strikes, bringing him perilously close to termination. Eventually, Kovan managed to secure a transfer to a store nearer to his home, providing a glimmer of hope and relief.

As Kovan and Taneesha's love and commitment deepened, their journey took an unexpected turn. A phone call during Kovan's lunch break at his new job would lead them to embark on a new chapter of their lives, one that required immense compassion, strength, and love. The voice on the other end of the line belonged to a social worker, reaching out on behalf of Kovan's half-sister, who was struggling with addiction and unable to provide a stable environment for her two children. It was a heartbreaking situation, with the potential of the kids being placed in foster care.

Kovan, discussed the situation with Taneesha. Recognizing the importance of keeping siblings together and providing them with a safe and loving home, they made the heartfelt decision to bring the children into their lives.

Taneesha's unwavering support and understanding were a testament to the strength of their bond. Together, they opened their hearts and home to the two young souls in need. They created a nurturing and stable environment, where love, patience, and understanding thrived. Welcoming the children into their family required adjustments and sacrifices, but Kovan and Taneesha embraced the challenge with unwavering determination. With open arms, they offered stability, care, and guidance to the little ones, providing them with a second chance at a brighter future.

POEM

Did I make the wrong move by bringing these kids in?
Did I go and ruin my life, do I know what I'm do-in
If these kids mess up my house, do you know that I'm sue-in
Yeah, I know it's been awhile since you heard from me
I've been stuck with these two kids…State of emergency
They went and threw them on us like we had bionic shoulders
No help, no check, things are getting colder

They wanted their home to become a sanctuary, a place where love, understanding, and healing would prevail. Kovan and Taneesha navigate the complexities of parenting together, learning and growing alongside their new additions. They provided a safe space for the children to flourish, offering them stability, support, and the unconditional love they had longed for.

Through it all, Kovan and Taneesha's bond remained unwavering. Their shared journey, once centered on their love for each other, now extended to include the love and care they poured into the lives of the two innocent souls entrusted to them.

With each passing day, Kovan and Taneesha would celebrate the joys and milestones of their blended family, cherishing the precious moments and trying to build a future filled with love, hope, and endless possibilities. And through it all, they remained eternally grateful for the strength of their bond, the love they shared, and the extraordinary journey they embarked upon as husband and wife.

As Kovan and Taneesha welcomed Que and Anjie into their home, they soon realized that their new journey would come with its own set of unique challenges. While their hearts overflowed with love for the children, they began to notice some concerning behaviors.

Que, the one-year-old boy, struggled with communication. Instead of using words, he would resort to persistent screaming whenever he desired something. This communication barrier was a source of frustration for both him and his caregivers. Despite their best efforts, they couldn't decipher his needs or help him express himself effectively.

To their surprise, the social worker had neglected to disclose any information about Que's developmental challenges. This omission left Kovan and Taneesha feeling overwhelmed and ill-prepared to address his specific needs. However, their determination and commitment to providing the best possible care for Que did not waver.

Meanwhile, Anjie, Que's five-year-old sister, had picked up some negative habits during her time living with her mother. The instability she experienced early in life had left its mark, and she carried emotional scars that manifested in certain behaviors. Kovan and Taneesha recognized the importance of providing her with stability, structure, and a nurturing environment to help her heal and grow.

Understanding the complex dynamics at play, Kovan and Taneesha sought additional support. They reached out to professionals who specialized in early childhood development and behavior management. Through therapy and counseling, they learned strategies to better communicate with Que, helping him gradually develop more effective ways of expressing himself.

Simultaneously, Kovan and Taneesha worked diligently with Anjie to establish routines, boundaries, and positive reinforcement techniques. They provided a safe and loving environment that they hoped would allow her to unlearn negative behaviors and develop healthier coping mechanisms.

Their journey as parents to Que and Anjie demanded unwavering patience, understanding, and compassion. Kovan and Taneesha found strength in their love for the children, their commitment to their well-being, and their unyielding determination to provide them with the best opportunities in life.

As the days turned into weeks and the weeks into months, Que began to make remarkable progress. With the support of speech therapy and the consistent love and care of his new family, he gradually started to use words to express his needs and emotions. Kovan and Taneesha celebrated each milestone as a testament to Que's resilience and their unwavering dedication.

Though their journey was not without its challenges, Kovan and Taneesha remained steadfast in their dedication to Que and Anjie. They believed that every child deserves a chance at a bright future, and they were determined to provide just that. As Taneesha and

Kovan adjusted to their expanding family, they received news that would further change the dynamics of their household. They discovered that they were expecting a baby of their own, adding another layer of excitement and anticipation to their lives.

However, their joy was tempered by an unexpected turn of events. Kovan lost his job due to a strict policy regarding lunch breaks. Just three months into his new position, he received his third strike and was abruptly terminated. The drive home was a somber and tearful journey, with Kovan contemplating what he would say to his wife, Taneesha, about the unfortunate turn of events.

Taneesha's loving support was a beacon of light for Kovan during his darkest times. As he navigated the challenges of unemployment and the emotional toll of losing his job, Taneesha stood by his side with unwavering love and understanding. She recognized the immense pressure he had been under, driving long hours to and from work and fearing for his safety on the road. Her presence and empathy provided the emotional stability that Kovan needed to face his situation with strength and hope.

In the days following his termination, Taneesha encouraged Kovan to take some time for himself, to process his feelings and emotions. She assured him that they were in this together and that they would find a way to overcome this setback. She reminded him of his talents, skills, and the years of dedication he had given to his former company, making it clear that his worth extended far beyond that job.

While Kovan searched for new job opportunities, Taneesha handled the financial aspect with care, understanding the importance of balancing their resources during this transitional period. Her support not only alleviated the burden on Kovan but also provided him the space and confidence to explore new possibilities without feeling overwhelmed.

Throughout the job hunt, Taneesha stayed up late with Kovan, revising his resume and crafting cover letters, always offering words of encouragement and reassurance. Her belief in his abilities was a constant source of motivation, reminding him of his strengths and encouraging him to pursue roles that truly aligned with his passions.

As they both actively sought employment, they discovered new facets of their relationship. The teamwork they exhibited during this period brought them even closer, and their shared determination to overcome challenges solidified their bond. They attended job fairs together, helping each other prepare for interviews, and celebrating each small victory along the way.

With Taneesha's support, Kovan's mental health remained stable, avoiding the path of despair that could have easily consumed him. He appreciated her willingness to listen without judgment and her ability to lift his spirits even on the most difficult days. Their love proved to be an anchor during this storm, providing the strength and resilience they needed to weather the uncertainties.

Despite the setback, Kovan embraced his role as a stay-at-home dad while waiting to hear back from an employer with a sense of purpose and dedication. He took on the responsibility of getting the children ready for school, ensuring the house was clean, and managing the daily chores.

POEM

Someone's got it in for me I'm not going to let them succeed though
Someone's got it in for me I'm not going to let them succeed though
Someone's got it in for me I'm not going to let them succeed
They're trying to bring me down slowly man you wouldn't believe
What I go through, on any given day, no play
Not any given Sunday, I'm talking every single day
They want to see me give up but I will never lie down
Everyday I show up they're always wearing a frown
I just smile, like wow, what are you going to do now
I saw you put on that frown so I'll just keep up this smile
They're trying to hold me back from climbing start to the top
But like Bad Boy Imma tell you that I just won't stop
Yo I'm never gone drop forever holding my spot
So what the temperatures hot You want me to give up; I'm not
Your word's not meaning a lot. Want me to jump off the dock?
They're steady buying different keys I'm steady picking the lock
Someone's got it in for me I'm not going to let them succeed though
There's some people out to kill… I ain't play-in
First degree understand me… I'm just saying
They blocked my transfer when I was trying to get home
I drove an hour to work; woke up on the side of the road
I went out looking for an opening all on my own

Windy Road

I didn't even consonant them, they said I was wrong
I stepped on people's toes that 's what they said
When my transfer came man their face turned red
Face turned red; face turned red
Someone's got it in for me I'm not going to let them succeed though
Someone's got it in for me I'm not going to let them succeed though
Look as I sit here without a job times get hard
I struggle to put gas in my car this has gotta be wrong
No weaknesses, so I've got to stay strong
Take care of my home feet to the street, I'm getting to on
This sounds like a song it's been a month as throw me a bone
Insurance is gone I remember when my paychecks were long
This has gotta be wrong wife's by my side so I'm not alone
I've got to stay strong survived from soft words on the phone
Someone's got it in for me I'm not going to let them succeed though
Someone's got it in for me I'm not going to let them succeed though

CHAPTER 12:

ADDITIONS AND SUBTRACTIONS

During this time, Anjie expressed a desire to stay with Kovan's mother, drawn to the presence of her older sister and the companionship of other children. Recognizing the importance of maintaining stability and a sense of familiarity for Anjie, Kovan and Taneesha agreed to let her live with Kovan's mother. Simultaneously, Kovan's half-sister faced yet another challenge in her life as she had another baby, only to have the child removed from her care and placed with Kovan's mom due to her ongoing struggles with addiction. With the unexpected turn of events, Kovan and Taneesha said that they would take the newborn, and his mom would take Anjie. Kovan's mother said she would take on both kids.

As Kovan embraced his role as a dedicated father and caretaker, Taneesha sought new employment opportunities. She was determined to continue contributing to their family's financial stability and providing for their expanding needs. Together, they navigated the challenges of unemployment and worked as a team to ensure the well-being of Que and their unborn baby. Months passed, and amidst the ups and downs of life, Taneesha found a new job, bringing a renewed sense of stability to their household. With their family dynamics evolving once again, Kovan and Taneesha continued to prioritize open communication and adaptability as they prepared for the arrival of their own baby.

As Taneesha's pregnancy progressed, Kovan's excitement and anticipation grew with each passing day. Despite the challenges of being out of work, he found solace in being able to attend all of Taneesha's doctor appointments, cherishing the opportunity to witness the miracle of their growing baby firsthand. With every visit to the doctor, Kovan's mind would drift back to their high school days, reflecting on the twists and turns that eventually led them to this moment. He couldn't help but feel a sense of awe and gratitude that their paths had crossed once again, resulting in a deep and meaningful connection that blossomed into a loving marriage and the impending arrival of their child.

As Taneesha's baby bump grew larger, Kovan found himself captivated by the wonder of it all. He would gently rub her belly, feeling the gentle movements of their little one, and it filled him with an indescribable joy. The bond they shared as expectant parents strengthened with each flutter and kick, creating a deep sense of connection between them and their unborn child. In those moments, Kovan realized the profound responsibility and privilege that awaited him as a father. He felt a mixture of excitement, nervousness, and a deep sense of love for life growing inside Taneesha's womb. He embraced the role of an expectant father wholeheartedly, eagerly preparing for the new chapter that was about to unfold in their lives.

POEM

You're shining just a little bit brighter now
I look into your eyes and smile, we're about to have a child
Man I'm so proud, can't hold it in... Let's scream and shout
Tell the world, cause baby you're my special girl
A boy or girl to raise right in this dangerous world
Little Keith or Naomi, how happy would I be?
Only my wife and kid because they're all that I see
I can't wait until I see you wobbling around the room
Stomach so big that you can't see your shoes
Throwing up my food, man I think that's rude
You know I understand, let me clean up the mess
Come here so I can say a few things in your ear
I'm fine and feeling good just as long as you're near
Listen here; sit back as I battle your fears
No tears just happy cheers like Barney with a beer
I want to rub your stomach until the end of time
I going to be there every second to make sure you're fine
Whatever you need no matter cause I'm up to the deed
I got to succeed I promise cause you carry my seed
I want to hear my baby's heart beat so come close to my ear
As soon as I hear a sound it just might bring me to tears

Rain On A Beautiful Day

Hi baby can you hear me in there
I'm so excited to see you I feel it all through my hair
I've got my hands on mommy's stomach so I can feel you move
You have music going on because I can feel you grove
We play tag on mommy's stomach as she lay and relax
I go and tap on mommy's stomach that's when you tag me back
Now there you go running from me
Come on back up because on top is where I need you to be
There you are…oh no see you're running again
Come back up so you can feel my heartbeat through my hands

As the due date approached, Kovan and Taneesha made preparations to welcome their baby into the world. They transformed a room in their home into a cozy nursery, filled with love and anticipation. They carefully selected tiny clothes, assembled a crib, and arranged toys and books, eagerly awaiting the day when their bundle of joy would arrive. Throughout this journey, Kovan couldn't help but marvel at the miracles of life and the incredible journey they

had embarked upon together. From their high school days to the present moment, their love had endured, evolved, and blossomed into a profound connection that would now extend to their precious child.

As they prepared to become parents, Kovan and Taneesha leaned on each other for support, drawing strength from their shared love and commitment. They knew that their lives were about to change in ways they couldn't fully comprehend, but they faced the future with open hearts and a deep sense of gratitude.

The anticipation and nerves reached their peak as Taneesha prepared for the arrival of their baby, Ennovy. However, things didn't go as smoothly as they had hoped during the delivery process. Initially, the doctor sent Taneesha and Kovan back home because she hadn't dilated enough. Taneesha's mother, concerned about the family history of difficulty in giving birth naturally due to their smaller stature, had tried to convey this information to the nurses.

Eventually, they returned to the hospital, and it became clear to the doctor that Taneesha's mother's concerns were valid. Taneesha's dilation still hadn't progressed enough, and a cesarean section was deemed necessary. As Taneesha was being prepped for the procedure, one of the nurses, who was responsible for administering the anesthesia, told her to alert him if she felt anything so he could sedate her further.

Taneesha, conscious of her past surgery to remove her appendix, attempted to communicate this to the nurse as they began the incision. However, before she could fully convey her concerns, she was swiftly and deeply sedated. Kovan stood by Taneesha's side, anxiously waiting for their baby to make their grand entrance into the world.

As Taneesha lay peacefully under anesthesia, Kovan was the first to lay eyes on their newborn daughter, Ennovy. He was overcome with a mixture of emotions as he gazed at their little bundle of joy. With each precious feature and tiny breath, a wave of love washed over Kovan's heart. He marveled at the miracle of new life and felt an overwhelming sense of gratitude for the safe arrival of their baby girl.

Though Taneesha couldn't be there in those initial moments, Kovan held Ennovy close, cherishing the connection they shared. He knew that Taneesha would be thrilled and eager to meet their daughter as soon as she woke up from the anesthesia. Hours later, as Taneesha slowly regained consciousness, she was greeted by the sight of Kovan cradling their precious Ennovy in his arms. Joy and relief washed over her as she finally laid eyes on their daughter, the culmination of their love and the beginning of a new chapter in their lives. But were they ready to face the world and create a future filled with love, hope, and endless possibilities?

POEM

Got to tell you what you mean to me
Without your love my life is empty
Like my lungs with no air to breathe
You lead my heart like a symphony
Love you from A-Z
You're down to earth and you're so unique
Girl I love our chemistry
When I feel low you are the energy, feeding me
The first time I laid eyes on you

Rain On A Beautiful Day

I didn't know what to do I was surprised by you
You had me so confused
The first time I laid eyes on you
I didn't know what to do I was surprised by you
You had me so confused
Baby you were there to hold my head after we lost the game
You wiped my tears and killed my fears
And help me through the pain
Where would I be if I didn't have you in my life right now
Where would I be if I couldn't turn around and see your smile
Where would I be if you only lived in my dreams
And I would stay asleep so you could be with me
All night long eyes closed
My baby won't be left alone
My Nene won't be left alone
The first time I laid eyes on you
I didn't know what to do
I was surprised by you
You had me so confused
The first time I laid eyes on you
I didn't know what to do
This is my love letter
To my one and only true love
To the women who changed my life
To the women who saved my life

~ END ~

PREQUEL

TITLE: HOLD MY HAND

In a small town, lived a young boy named Kovan, whose days were filled with sorrow and tears. Abandoned by his father, he often found solace on the cold kitchen floor, where his tears became companions. His heart ached for the love and guidance of a father figure, but it seemed like an elusive dream.

One fateful day, a stranger arrived in town, emanating an air of wisdom and empathy. His name was Kovan, and he bore a secret. Future Kovan had traversed through time, compelled by an unseen force, to offer comfort and support to those in need. As he observed Kovan's tears, he knew he had come to the right place.

"Little man, get up off the floor and wipe your tears," Future Kovan spoke, his voice filled with kindness. "I've traveled back in time just to be here with you. You're not alone, for I can feel your fears. Let me take you home, where you will find solace in my embrace."

Younger Kovan's eyes widened in surprise and curiosity. How could this stranger understand his pain? It was as if they shared the same sorrowful journey. As they embarked on their walk home, Future Kovan revealed his own past, a tale of abandonment and loneliness that resonated deeply with younger Kovan. It was a bond forged through shared experiences.

With each passing day, Future Kovan became a guiding presence in younger Kovan's life. He understood why younger Kovan cried in secret, why he felt shame reflected in the mirror. Future Kovan yearned to offer hope, to tell younger Kovan that the pain would fade away, and that those who had caused his suffering would make amends. But honesty compelled him to admit the painful truth—they would not.

Younger Kovan's heart sank upon hearing this, yet younger Kovan's compassionate presence allowed him to see beyond the limitations of his circumstances. Through their shared journey, Future Kovan taught younger Kovan to find strength within himself, to rise above the hurt and the disappointment. He instilled in younger Kovan a sense of resilience and the understanding that his worth was not defined by the actions of others.

Together, they faced the disapproving whispers and indifferent glances of the townsfolk. Younger Kovan had often felt invisible, as though no one truly saw his tears or felt his fears. But Future Kovan saw him, truly and deeply, and encouraged him to embrace his emotions and express his pain to those who had hurt him. It was through this vulnerability that younger Kovan discovered a newfound strength, an unyielding resolve to stand tall in the face of adversity.

As the days turned into weeks, younger Kovan's tears diminished, replaced by a glimmer of hope in his eyes. With Future Kovan's unwavering support, he found the courage to confront his loved ones, to express the hurt they had caused, and to let them know that their actions had left scars on his soul.

Although the wounds couldn't be erased, younger Kovan realized that healing came not from their acknowledgment or redemption but from within himself. He learned that the place he truly belonged was not with those who let him down but within his own heart, where he could nurture his dreams and build his own path to strength and fulfillment.

With time, younger Kovan's wounds began to heal, and the weight of his past slowly lifted. The echoes of his tears faded as he embraced the love and support that Future Kovan had selflessly offered. Through their shared journey, younger Kovan discovered that the power to grow strong resided within himself, not dependent on the actions of others.

And so, their story continued, a tale of resilience and the enduring bond between a young boy and a time-traveling guardian. Together, they traversed the bumpy roads of life, knowing that the pain might never completely dissipate but believing that with love, understanding, and self-acceptance, they could create their own place

Poem: I Wish

Little man, get up off the floor and wipe your tears.
I've traveled back in time just to be here.
I'm here to say you're not alone; I can feel your fears.
And I'm here to take you home as I hold you near.
I know your pain; we've been going through the same thing.
Know you're afraid cause our pain hits the same way.
Know why you cry on the side when you play games.
You disappear in the mirror cause you feel shame.

Wish I could tell you that the pain will move on.
Wish I could tell you that they'll right all their wrongs.
But they don't.
Wish I could tell you there's a place you belong.
Wish I could tell you that you and your pops would grow strong.
But y'all won't.
Wish I could tell you that the pain will move on.
Wish I could tell you that they'll right all their wrongs.
But they don't.
Wish I could tell you there's a place you belong.
Wish I could tell you that you and your pops would grow strong.
But y'all won't.

I know you feel like everybody let you down,
Like they didn't see your tears when they came around.
Like they couldn't feel your fears on this side of town,
Only cheers and cracking beers is the sound you found.
I saw you crying on the kitchen floor.
Wish you could open up a little more.
So you can tell them that they hurt you so.
Wish I could tell you that the pain will move on.
Wish I could tell you that they'll right all their wrongs.
But they don't.
Wish I could tell you there's a place you belong.
Wish I could tell you that you and your pops would grow strong.
But y'all won't.
Wish I could tell you that the pain will move on.
Wish I could tell you that they'll right all their wrongs.
But they don't.

Wish I could tell you there's a place you belong.
Wish I could tell you that you and your pops would grow strong.
But y'all won't.
Wish I could tell you there's a place you belong.
Wish I could tell you that you and your pops would grow strong.
Wish I could tell you there's a place you belong.
Wish I could tell you that you and your pops would grow strong.
But y'all won't.

TITLE: THE UNSPOKEN CONNECTION

In the housing projects of Pasadena, CA, lived two brothers, each living in their own separate worlds. The younger brother, Kovan, looked up to his older sibling, Kenneth, with admiration and a yearning for connection. But it seemed that every time Kovan reached out, Kenneth was already gone, engrossed in his own endeavors.

Kovan couldn't comprehend the meaning behind his brother's constant absence. Whenever he believed he had a moment of Kenneth's undivided attention, his hopes were dashed as Kenneth was already involved in some other venture, constantly on the move. Kovan longed for his brother's guidance, for him to translate the complexities of the world.

With a seven-year age gap, Kenneth seemed like he resided in an entirely different realm, a whole other home. He had achieved great success, proudly displaying trophies on his wall, particularly in sports where he excelled. Kovan believed that when he reached high school, Kenneth would help him flourish, show him the path to success. However, fate had other plans.

Tragedy struck when Kenneth fell from grace, leaving Kovan feeling abandoned and alone. In moments of vulnerability, Kovan looked into the stands during his athletic pursuits, hoping to find his brother's reassuring presence. Yet, no one was there to offer a supportive hand or to understand the challenges Kovan faced.

The weight of the challenges on the field crushed Kovan's spirit, threatening to extinguish his dreams. If only his brother had stayed, if only he hadn't left him alone, perhaps things would have been different. But in the absence of his brother's support, Kovan found strength within himself. He realized that he could carry the weight of his dreams and ambitions, even without his brother's presence.

Kovan yearned to be like his older brother, to don his number and emulate his success, but he soon discovered that he couldn't fill Kenneth's shoes. He couldn't capture the attention of the fans or replicate the adulation that his brother had received. Kovan felt lost, constantly compared to his brother's achievements, feeling like he could never measure up.

While Kenneth was protected and cherished by those around him, Kovan stood alone, facing the challenges and hardships on his own. He had been left in the dirt, feeling deserted. However, amidst the pain and loneliness, Kovan found resilience and an unwavering determination to forge his path. He refused to let the absence of his brother define his worth.

Sibling rivalry weighed heavily on Kovan's heart, an unspoken competition that shadowed their relationship. Yet, Kovan realized that it was time to shift the spotlight to himself. No matter what game they played, Kovan decided that it was his time to shine. He would show the world his talents, his worth, and prove that he was more than just Kenneth's shadow.

As the story continued, Kovan embarked on a journey of self-discovery and perseverance. He faced numerous obstacles and setbacks, but he refused to give in. The absence of his brother's support fueled his determination, propelling him forward. With every challenge he conquered, he found strength within himself, realizing that he was capable of greatness in his own right.

And so, Kovan embraced his individuality, defying the expectations set by his brother's success. He learned to overcome the comparisons and the longing for his brother's presence. With each victory, he carved his path, leaving behind a legacy that was uniquely his own.

In the end, the unbreakable bond between the brothers remained, transcending the physical distance and the disparities in their journeys. Kovan's strength and resilience were a testament to the enduring connection they shared, even when they seemed worlds apart.

Poem: Big Brother

A big brother, somebody tell me what it means.
As soon as I turn, he's gone, always cruising the scene.

When I think his time is mine, he's into some other thing,
Some other scheme, big brother, translate for me.
I should have known he's always gone,
Rarely at home; why would he have time for me?
Man, he's almost grown, a seven-year difference, yeah,
And in a whole other zone, a whole other home.
Big brother, throw me a bone.
He had trophies on the wall; dang, he could ball.
Soon as I get to high school, he will help me to ball.
But who knew he would fall and leave me there all alone?
I looked in the stands, yo, there's nobody there.
I blinked my eyes three times again, looked in the stands,
But nowhere was my man, no one to give me a hand,
No one that could understand what I was going through, man.
The challenges on the field that really killed my will,
I knew my dream was gone when I stood there all alone.
If my brother was never gone, I wouldn't have this song.
If he hadn't left me alone, I wouldn't be this strong
To carry the throne; seems like I'm best on my own.
I tried to don his number to be like Superman;
I couldn't be my big brother; I couldn't rock the fans.
I couldn't rock the fans; I couldn't understand.
Everybody supported him; I swear him lived in the gym.
They protected him like a shield as he played on the field,
Kept him from falling down as he stood on the mound.
But look at me now; I look around, and no one's around.
Was I hurt? Sure, I was hurt; I was left in the dirt,
Feeling deserted; look what you've done to the kid.
It's like I never can win; it's like I never fit in,
Kicked over and over again, but I will never give in.
Sibling rivalry, yeah, it's tough as can be,
Since he had all the glory, then it's time to shift it to me.
Whatever we play, no matter 'cause it's my way today,
My way today, kill him at whatever we play.

Title: Shadows of the Hood

In a gritty neighborhood plagued by poverty and crime, young Kovan found himself caught in the harsh realities of his environment. The hood, with its endless cycle of violence and despair, became his twisted playground. Every day, people fell victim to robberies and violence, creating an atmosphere of fear and mistrust.

As Kovan observed the chaos around him, he couldn't help but wish for a change, a respite from the constant danger that loomed. Bullet shells scattered the streets, testifying to the rampant gunfire that pierced the air. Drug addicts roamed the neighborhood, their desperate pleas for more serving as a haunting reminder of the grip of addiction.

The little glimmer of hope in children's eyes seemed to fade away, replaced by a sense of hopelessness. Kovan understood the bleak reality that surrounded them, the absence of opportunity and a better future. It was a vicious cycle that seemed impossible to escape.

In this unforgiving world, Kovan knew he had to be prepared to defend himself, with everyone carrying guns, a means of survival in a landscape where fools preyed on others' weaknesses. But the more he delved into this world of violence, the more he realized that the gun he wielded could easily turn against him.

Gunshots echoed through the air, a constant reminder of the indifference that permeated the neighborhood. Before venturing out at night, Kovan whispered prayers, hoping for protection from the evil that lurked in the shadows. But the darkness seemed to have a way of finding its victims, stripping away any sense of security.

The streets became a merciless arena, where danger awaited at every corner. Kovan witnessed firsthand the devastating consequences that befell those who ignored the warnings. Families mourned the loss of their loved ones, left with a void that could never be filled.

Amidst the chaos, Kovan tried desperately to protect his name, to keep his credit in the eyes of the community intact. But external forces conspired against him, tearing him apart from within. Betrayed by someone he trusted, he felt his identity crumble under false accusations.

Lost and alone, Kovan searched for solace, for any sign that his voice still mattered. But his cries fell on deaf ears, drowning in the silence that surrounded him. He knew he had to gather the shattered pieces of his spirit and find the strength to rise above the darkness that threatened to consume him.

These were his ghetto dreams, the aspirations suffocated by the harsh realities of his upbringing. The screams of children echoed through the streets, a collective cry for salvation, for a chance to break free from the chains that bound them.

But amidst the despair, Kovan vowed to defy the odds. He would not let the circumstances define him. With resilience and determination, he fought to reclaim his voice, to rewrite his story. He knew that the struggle was far from over, but he refused to let the hood's shadows consume him entirely.

And as the screams of children echoed in the distance, Kovan vowed to be their voice, to break the cycle of despair and pave the way for a brighter future. He carried the weight of their dreams, their hopes, and he would not rest until their screams transformed into laughter and their dreams became a reality.

Poem: Ghetto Dreams

It's suicide no truth but lies when you live in the hood
People get robbed every day but I wish they would
I saw people dropped on their face when they got out of place
I saw bullet shells on the floor, multiple holes through the door
Now tell me I'm wrong; my playground's infested, my horse
Got crack fiends on the corner begging for more and more
Got naked addicts through the neighborhood, high off that fresh
dope
Look in little kids' eyes and see that there's no hope
Nope, no one's gonna come for you; tell me what you're going to
do.
Keep the pain in front of you, carrying a gun or two

For fools who fronts on you, then you get to busting fools
What you gonna do when that gun seems to turn around on you?
Gunshots in the air, people really don't care
Before you go out at night, you better say your prayers
Beware, don't be afraid, or the Devil's gonna get you
You try to hide inside; he'll come and evict you
Pistol-whip you; your family's gonna miss you
They warned you to stay out the streets 'cause it'll hit you
Your family's gonna—
You better beware of the darkness 'cause it'll snatch you
You better beware of the darkness 'cause it'll attack you
When the sun goes down, boy, you better run home
When the street lights come on, you better hit the floor
Before you hear screams
This is my childhood story
I tried so hard to keep my credit all good
It seems outside forces quickly took me out to the woods
She beat my name down to the ground; now it's no longer found
I'm searching and looking alone but still not hearing a sound
I can't fathom how she could really truly do me this way
She served me up to the wolves on a fallacious tray
There's no way I can stay; I need to pick myself up
There's no other way around it, man; what she did was corrupt
These are my ghetto dreams
These are why kids scream
These are my ghetto dreams
This is why kids scream
Title: Silent Battles

Kovan sat alone in his room, tears welling up inside him, but never finding their way down his cheeks. He felt invisible, as if the people around him couldn't see the pain that consumed him. His fears lurked deep within his mind, hidden from the outside world.

Lost and confused, Kovan felt like he was wandering aimlessly, searching for a place where he truly belonged. He felt disconnected from his surroundings, as if he had forgotten his past, as if he had never been a carefree child. The weight of his emotions pressed heavily on him, leaving him feeling suffocated.

"He longed for reassurance, for someone to tell him that everything would be okay, even if it was a lie. He yearned for a sense of stability in his tumultuous world. His heart quivered with anxiety, sending tremors through his being, darker than any birthday he had experienced.

The blinds of his mind remained closed, blocking out the sunlight that could bring warmth and clarity. His thoughts were trapped, the key to unlocking his mind just out of reach. He craved peace, an escape from the incessant turmoil that kept him awake at night.

His body moved freely through the physical world, but his mind felt imprisoned, confined to a jail of its own making. He longed for release, but it seemed impossible to break free from the shackles that held his thoughts captive. The air around him was fresh, yet he couldn't seem to draw it into his lungs.

Kovan questioned himself, wondering if he was truly wrong for feeling this way. He yearned for connection, fearing the prospect of being alone. The world seemed cold and unforgiving as he drove down the empty road of his existence.

He often found himself preoccupied with the opinions of others, caring too much about what they thought of him. It felt as if his mind and body were conspiring against him, betraying him at every turn. He sought solace in solitude, but even in his moments of seclusion, sorrow managed to find him.

Kovan kept his emotions locked away, as they had a tendency to escalate rapidly from a two to a ten. He likened himself to a dormant monster, capable of unleashing a storm of emotions when provoked. Even his closest loved ones couldn't escape the cloud of darkness that hung over him.

In moments of desperation, Kovan found himself lying in bed, with a gun pointed straight at his head, contemplating the release it could provide. He struggled to breathe, as if the weight of the world rested on his chest. He screamed in his dreams, hoping to vanish from his own existence.

He sought relief in pills, finding temporary respite from his internal struggles. The pharmacy became his refuge, a place where he could momentarily escape the chaos within. But the escape was fleeting, leaving him longing for true healing.

Kovan questioned how he could heal in a world that seemed so selfish and uncaring. It devoured people whole, treating them as mere commodities. He wondered how he was supposed to cope when those in power seemed to hold all the cards.

Yet, amidst the darkness, there remained a glimmer of hope within Kovan. He knew deep down that he had the strength to navigate his way through the labyrinth of his mind. He refused to let the world's callousness extinguish his spirit. With every breath, he fought to heal, to find solace in the midst of chaos, and to rise above the struggles that threatened to consume him.

Poem: Silent Pain

I'm crying inside… but never shed a tear
People outside my mind don't really know my fears
I don't know where I'm going… don't belong here
I forgot where I've been… like I never been a kid
Tell me it's go be okay on my worst day
Tell me that I'll be just fine even if you're lyin'
Tell me why my heart shakes like an earthquake
Darker than my B-day put on back on replay
I can't open the blinds to see the sunshine
I can't open my mind because the keys high
Out of reach it won't even let me seek a peek
I want peace so hopefully I can get some sleep
Body's free… but my mind trapped-in-jail
Release me… but I can't seem to make bail
Fresh air… but I can't seem to inhale
Have I failed… remove these cards that I was dealt
Tell me am I really wrong
I don't want to be alone
Man, this world is really cold
Driving on an empty road
Do I care too much about what people think of me
Sometimes I think my mind and body be betraying me

I try to go and be alone but it ain't meant to be
Hide and seek… mentally… sorrow keep on finding me
I stay reserved… cause my emotions go from 2 to 10
Call me the Hunk… cause a monster's sleeping deep within
Even my keen folk… can't even escape the smoke
Then I'm laying in the bed… gun pointing straight to my head
I can't breathe... can't seem... to stop these tears
When I scream... in my dreams… I disappear
When I feel… a little ill… another pill
Yo what's the deal… the pharmacy is my master kneel
Kill Bill wasn't real living in a movie reel
Tell me how I'm supposed to heal in a world that's selfish still
In a world that's full of thrills
Eat you up like you're the meal
Tell me how I'm supposed to deal
When the master got the power here."

Title: The Crossroads

J.T. stood at the crossroads of life, feeling the passing of time flowing around him. While others around him grew and evolved, he remained stagnant, trapped in a cycle of his own making. He had managed to escape the confines of the hood, moving to the suburbs, but his actions still reflected his troubled past.

Living on the wrong side of the tracks had taken its toll on J.T. He had lost sight of his dreams, feeling lost and devoid of purpose. The world seemed to conspire against him, pushing him further down a path of self-destruction. Yet, he held on, trying to find a way out of the darkness.

His old habits and negative influences were persistent, tempting Kovan to engage in sinful behaviors. But Kovan remained steadfast, refusing to succumb to the temptations that surrounded him. Kovan knew that the world was not meant for J.T., and he struggled to break free from its toxic grasp.

The realization dawned on him that he was living a lie. His actions were causing pain and suffering to his loved ones, yet he pushed them aside, blinded by his own selfish desires. His baby girl was growing up alone, deprived of a father's love and presence. The streets became his rhythm, a beat that he mindlessly followed, robbing others while ignoring the struggles they faced in their own lives.

Once a promising track star, J.T. had let his life become as fast-paced as his feet once were. His choices had transformed him into someone known as E.T., a persona far removed from his true self. The consequences of his actions finally caught up with him, as the secrets he had hidden for years came to light, exposing his true nature to those he held dear.

In a moment of reflection, J.T. was urged to press rewind, to revisit his childhood and remember the innocent joy he had once experienced. He was reminded of the immense stress his actions had placed on his mother and the impact it had on their family. And most importantly, he was forced to confront the repercussions of his choices on his daughter's life.

It was time for J.T. to make a decision. He had reached a turning point where he had to choose between the destructive path he had been on and the opportunity to create a better future for himself and his loved ones. With newfound clarity, he resolved to break free from the chains that held him captive, to rise above the temptations of his past, and to be there for his daughter, providing her with the love and guidance she deserved.

J.T. took a deep breath, ready to embark on a journey of redemption and growth. The passing of time would no longer be a reminder of his stagnation, but a measure of his progress. As he walked away from the crossroads, he embraced the hope that lay ahead, determined to create a new chapter in his life—one filled with love, responsibility, and the pursuit of a brighter future.

Poem: Time Passing

This passing time's flowing
You're stagnant, not growing
Got to get your mind up out of the hood
I see you moved to the burbs but still up to no good
This passing time's flowing
You're stagnant, not growing
Got to get your mind up out of the hood
I see you moved to the burbs but still up to no good
It's hard when you live on the wrong side of the tracks
He has no dreams, it seems he's lost, so toss him a map
He's lost his soul, he's cold and steady out of control
It seems like the world's against him, but he's trying to hold on
There you are again, acting like you're destined to won
You tried to pull me into sin but I'll never give in
The world's not for you, so what are you striving to do
It's poisoning your mind and you're not seeing the sign
Open your eyes and realize you're living a lie
Your loved ones are suffering as a result of your lies
But you don't mind that they cry, you just push them aside
You don't mind that they cry, you just push them aside
Your baby girl's alone because you're never at home

Marching to the streets as if the streets had a beat
Wake up, kid, you're something like a stickup kid
Robbing everybody when they're also struggling to live
This passing time's flowing
You're stagnant, not growing
Got to get your mind up out of the hood
I see you moved to the burbs but still up to no good
This passing time's flowing
You're stagnant, not growing
Got to get your mind up out of the hood
I see you moved to the burbs but still up to no good
A former track star whose life was as fast as his feet
My boy is no longer home; he's better known as JT
How could you do what you did when we went through it as kids
Oh yeah, you hid it for years, but now we're all your buzz
The next time you feel like lighting up, just press rewind
Back to a kid and how it had you feeling from dusk till dawn
If that doesn't work, think about the stress it put on your mom
No, wait, let's stop and see just how your daughter responds

~ The End ~